John R. Sweney

Songs of Love and Praise, no. 3

For Use in Meetings for Christian Worship or Work

John R. Sweney

Songs of Love and Praise, no. 3
For Use in Meetings for Christian Worship or Work

ISBN/EAN: 9783337182083

Printed in Europe, USA, Canada, Australia, Japan

Cover: Foto ©Thomas Meinert / pixelio.de

More available books at **www.hansebooks.com**

SONGS OF LOVE AND PRAISE,

— No. 3. —

FOR USE IN

MEETINGS FOR CHRISTIAN WORSHIP OR WORK.

EDITORS:

JOHN R. SWENEY, WM. J. KIRKPATRICK

AND H. L. GILMOUR.

"Love is the golden chain that binds the happy souls above."

JOHN J. HOOD,
PHILADELPHIA: CHICAGO:
1024 Arch St.   940 W. Madison St.

Copyright, 1896, by John J. Hood.

COPYRIGHT, 1896, BY JOHN J. HOOD.

THE love of God, all human love transcending,
　　Fondest and purest, sweetest and the best;
Without beginning, it shall have no ending,
　　Descending from, and leading to, the blest;
Royal—enrobed in all-enduring splendor,
　　Grieved by neglect, yet in forgiveness tender.

Bound, ransomed hearts! High joy excludes the sadness,
　　All tongues enthused, extol eternal love;
Enwreathed with smiles comes tripping sunlit gladness,
　　Each blessed note an echo from above·
While "Songs of Love and Praise," mingling together,
　　Increase the bliss of heaven, always, FOREVER!

　　　　　　　　　　　　　　　　　　　E. H. STOKES
Ocean Grove, N. J.

COPYRIGHT NOTICE.

To PRINT, for sale or otherwise, any copyright hymn of this collection, unless written permission shall have been obtained, is an infringement of copyright.

　　　　　　　　　　　　　　　　　　THE PUBLISHER.

— No. 3. —

Songs of Love and Praise.

1. Gloria Patri.

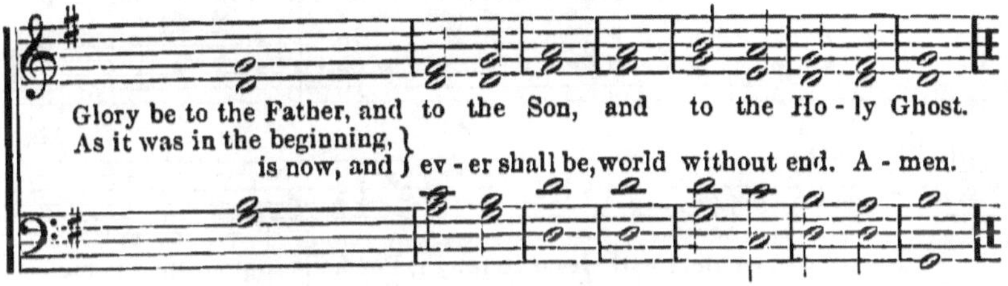

Glory be to the Father, and to the Son, and to the Ho-ly Ghost.
As it was in the beginning, is now, and ev-er shall be, world without end. A-men.

2. He is All in All to Me.

FANNY J. CROSBY.   Arr. by W. J. K.

1. There is constant joy a-biding In Christ my Lord and King; Of his love that
2. When my path is veil'd in shadows, And clouds above me roll, I can smile a-
3. I can see his bow of promise Thro' tears and trials deep; I can hear his
4. I shall yet behold and praise him, And dwell in per-fect peace In the golden

passeth knowledge My heart and tongue shall sing.
mid the tempest, His glory fills my soul.
voice like music, That lulls my care to sleep.
land of beauty, Where cloud and wave shall cease.

{ He is all in all to me,
{ And my song of songs shall be,

CHORUS.

he-is all in all to me,
my song of songs shall be,

Hal-le-lu-jah, O my Saviour, I am trusting on-ly thee.

Copyright, 1896, by Wm. J. Kirkpatrick.

Victory Everywhere.

Rev. M. M. Brabham.   Wm. J. Kirkpatrick.

1. Christian soldiers, why dismayed? Why let Sat-an make a-fraid?
2. E - vil arm - ies in their might Gather 'round and push the fight;
3. Armed and strengthened by his grace, We shall win in ev - 'ry place;
4. See our foes, a - way they fly, Je - sus Christ is com - ing nigh;

Je- sus Christ our cap - tain is, And the triumph must be his.
Loud and fierce they raise their cry, But be - fore our Lead- er fly.
Earth with hell in vain combines, Vic - t'ry on our ban - ner shines.
Death and sin be - fore him fall, Crown him Vic - tor o - ver all!

CHORUS.

Vic - to - ry, vic - to - ry everywhere, Christ our Lord shall triumph here!

Raise your voices high as heav'n; Vic - to - ry, vic - to - ry shall be giv'n.

Copyright, 1886, by Wm. J. Kirkpatrick.

Since I Have Been Redeemed.

E. O. E.
E. O. EXCELL. By per.

1. I have a song I love to sing, Since I have been redeemed, Of my Re-
2. I have a Christ that satis-fies, Since I have been redeemed, To do his
3. I have a Witness bright and clear, Since I have been redeemed, Dispelling
4. I have a joy I can't express, Since I have been redeemed, All thro' his
5. I have a home prepared for me, Since I have been redeemed, Where I shall

CHORUS.

deemer, Saviour King, Since I have been redeemed. Since I . . . have been re-
will my highest prize, Since I have been redeemed.
every doubt and fear, Since I have been redeemed.
blood and righteousness, Since I have been redeemed.
dwell e-ter-nal-ly, Since I have been redeemed. Since I have been redeemed, since

deemed, Since I have been redeemed, I will glory in his name, Since
I have been redeemed,

I . . . . have been redeemed, I will glory in the Saviour's name.
I have been redeemed, since I have been redeemed,

Copyright, 1884, by E. O. Excell.

2 When lost in sin, my all I squandered,
   Far from the fold:
My Saviour sought me where I wandered,
   Gave me his wealth untold.
All bonds of sin and Satan rending,
   Christ made me whole:
I'll ne'er forget that joy transcending,
   When Jesus saved my soul.

3 All round my way the sun is shining,
   Darkness has fled:
On Jesus' breast I am reclining,
   Daily by him I'm fed.
My Lord has cast his robe around me,
   No more I'll roam;
The Shepherd of the sheep has found me,
   Jesus has brought me home.

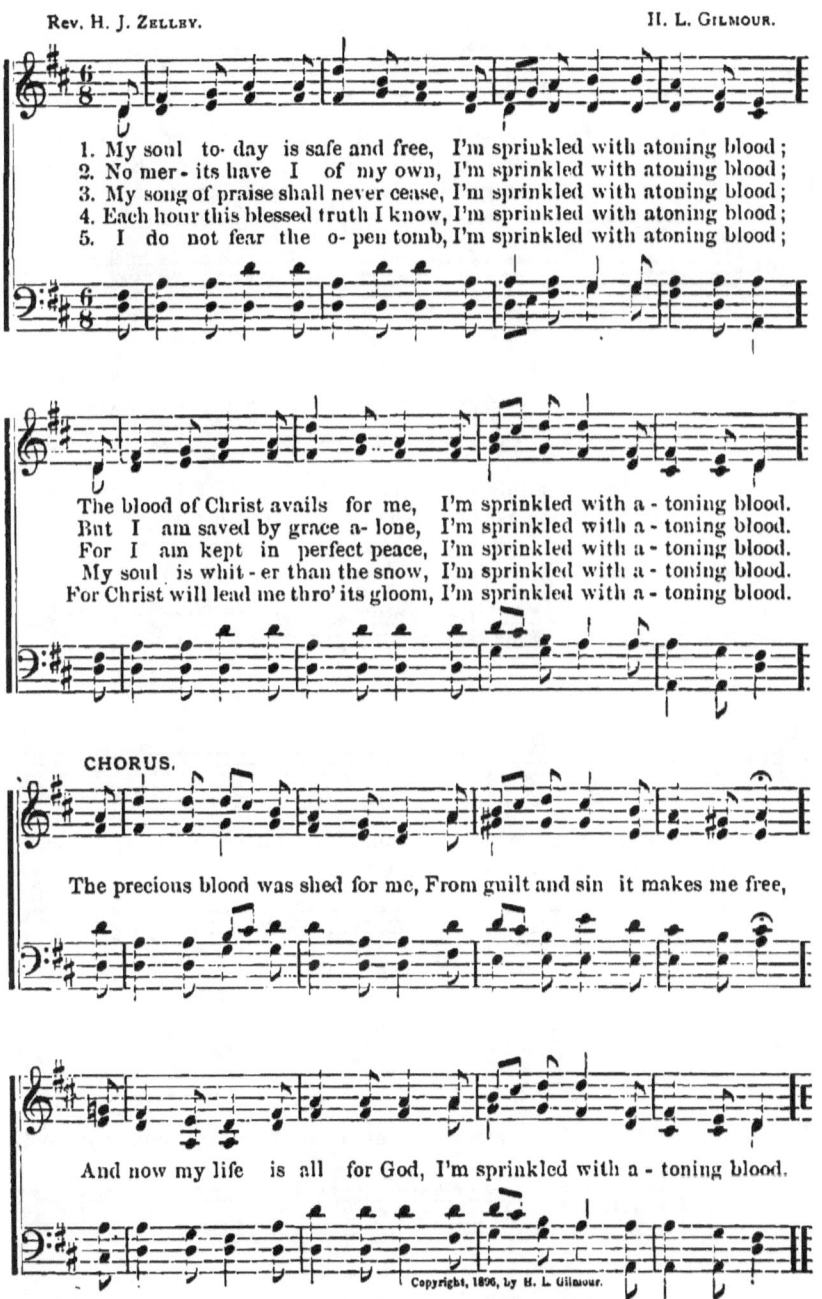

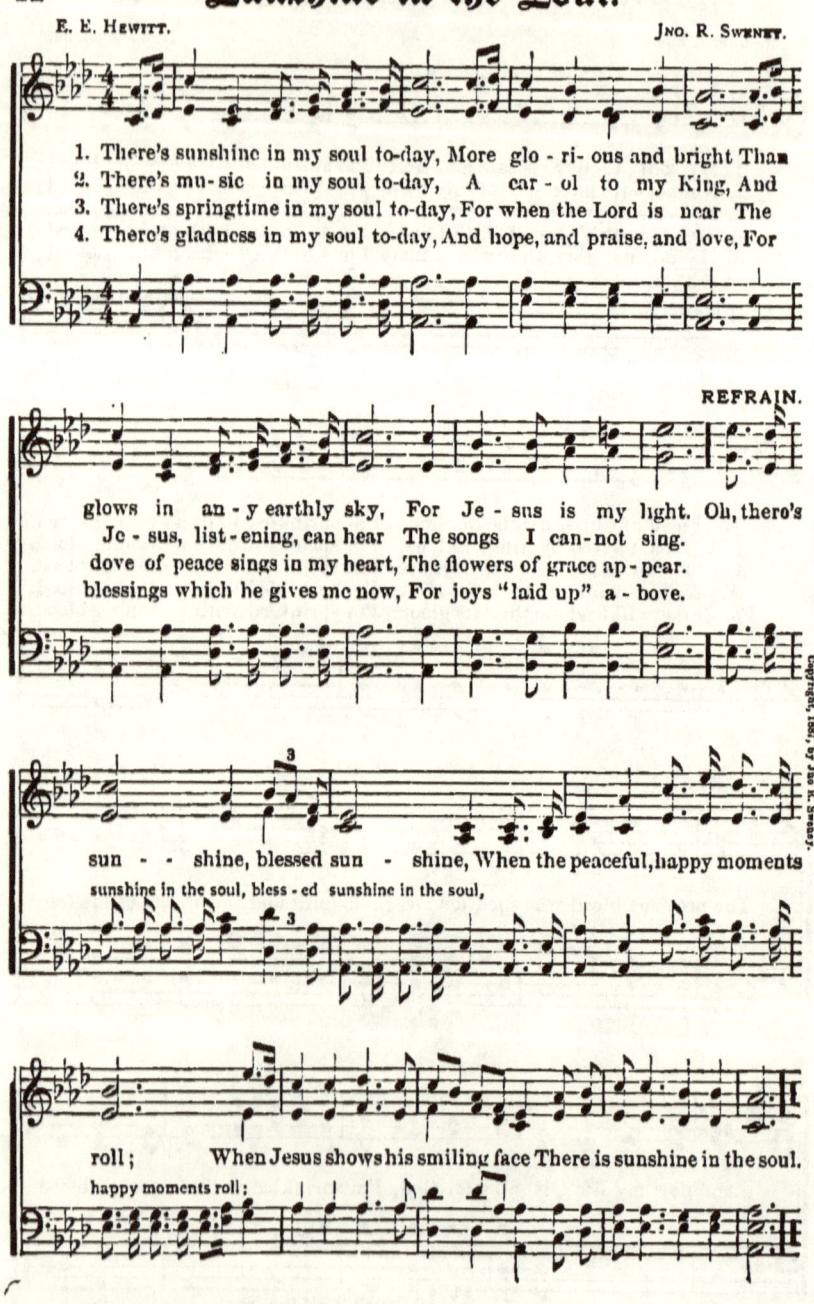

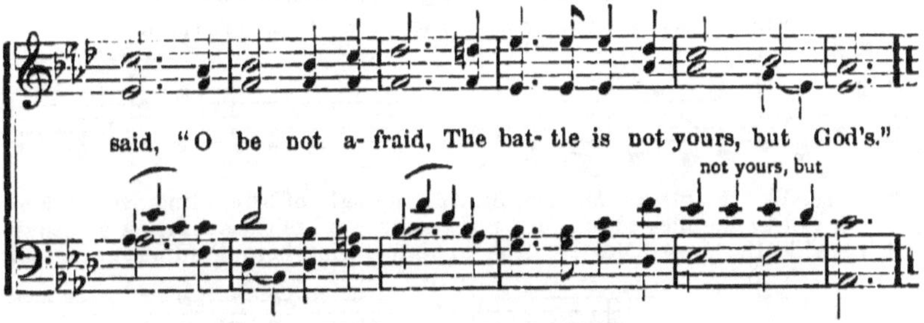

Victory Through Jesus.—CONCLUDED. 15

said, "O be not a-fraid, The bat-tle is not yours, but God's."

O Eden, Dear Eden.

FANNY J. CROSBY.   H. S. THOMPSON.

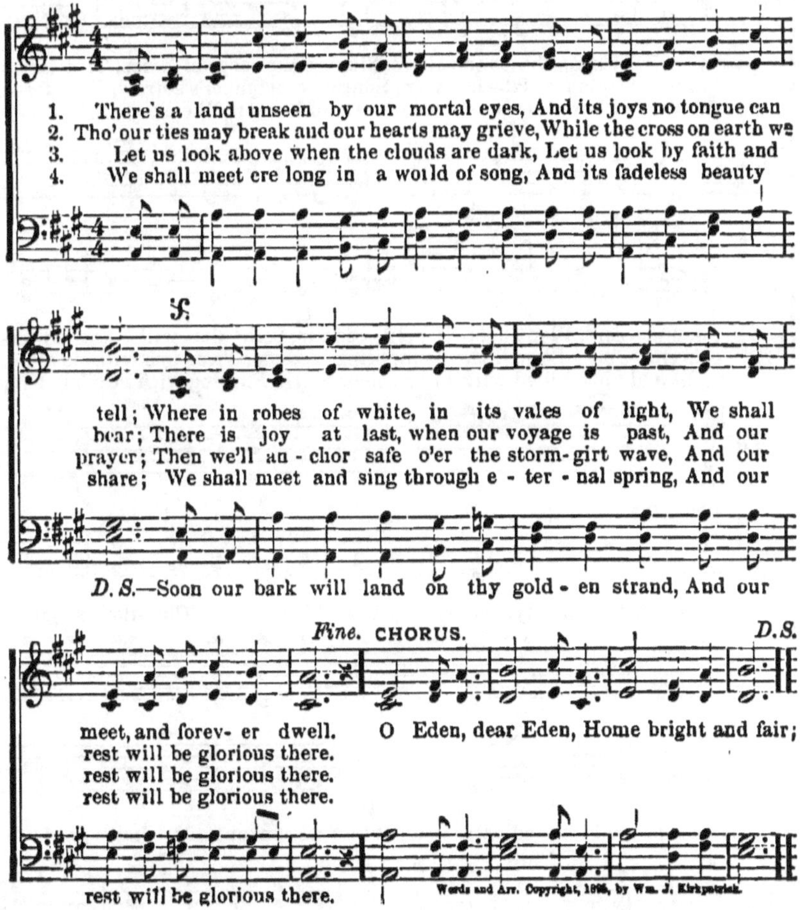

1. There's a land unseen by our mortal eyes, And its joys no tongue can
2. Tho' our ties may break and our hearts may grieve, While the cross on earth we
3. Let us look above when the clouds are dark, Let us look by faith and
4. We shall meet ere long in a world of song, And its fadeless beauty

tell; Where in robes of white, in its vales of light, We shall
bear; There is joy at last, when our voyage is past, And our
prayer; Then we'll an-chor safe o'er the storm-girt wave, And our
share; We shall meet and sing through e-ter-nal spring, And our

D. S.—Soon our bark will land on thy gold-en strand, And our

Fine. CHORUS.   *D. S.*

meet, and forev-er dwell.   O Eden, dear Eden, Home bright and fair;
rest will be glorious there.
rest will be glorious there.
rest will be glorious there.

rest will be glorious there.   Words and Arr. Copyright, 1895, by Wm. J. Kirkpatrick.

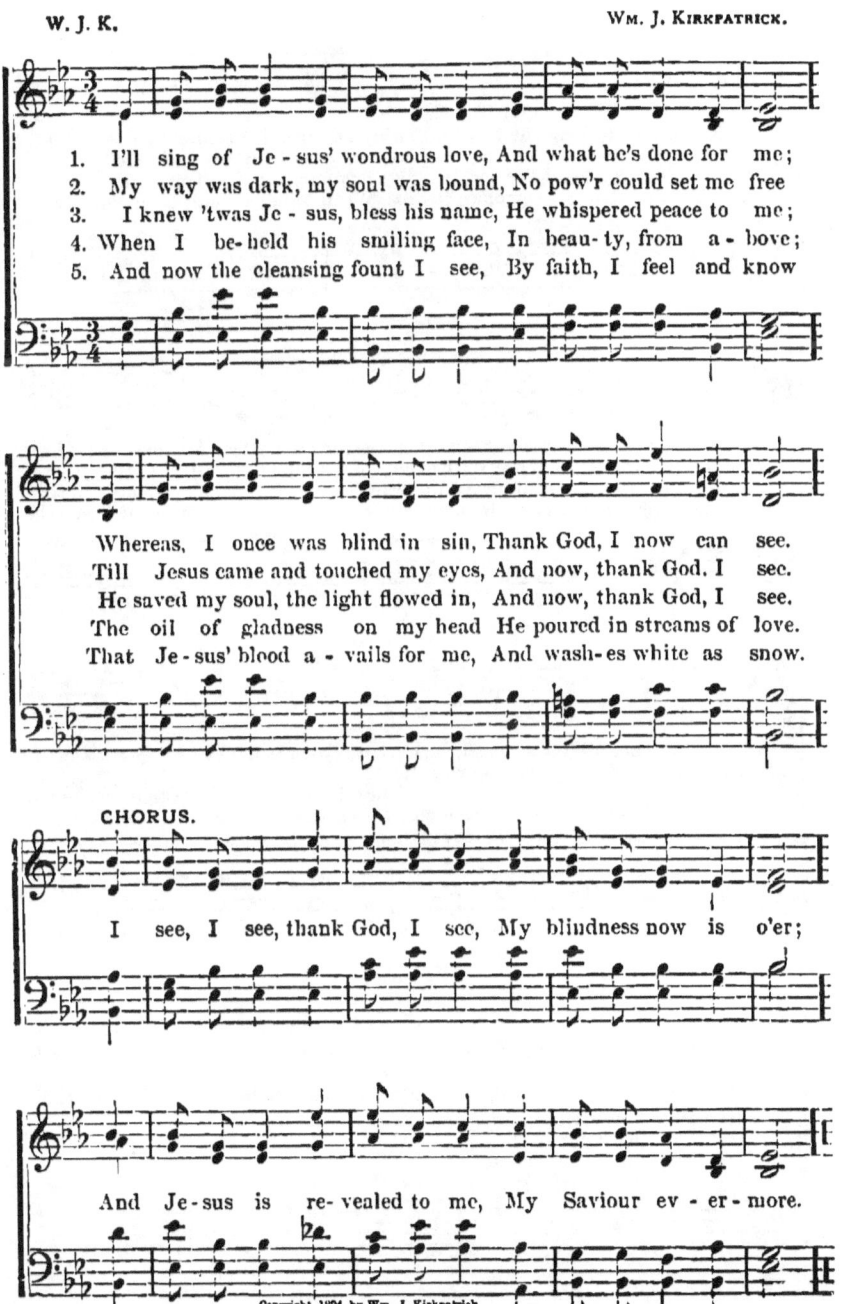

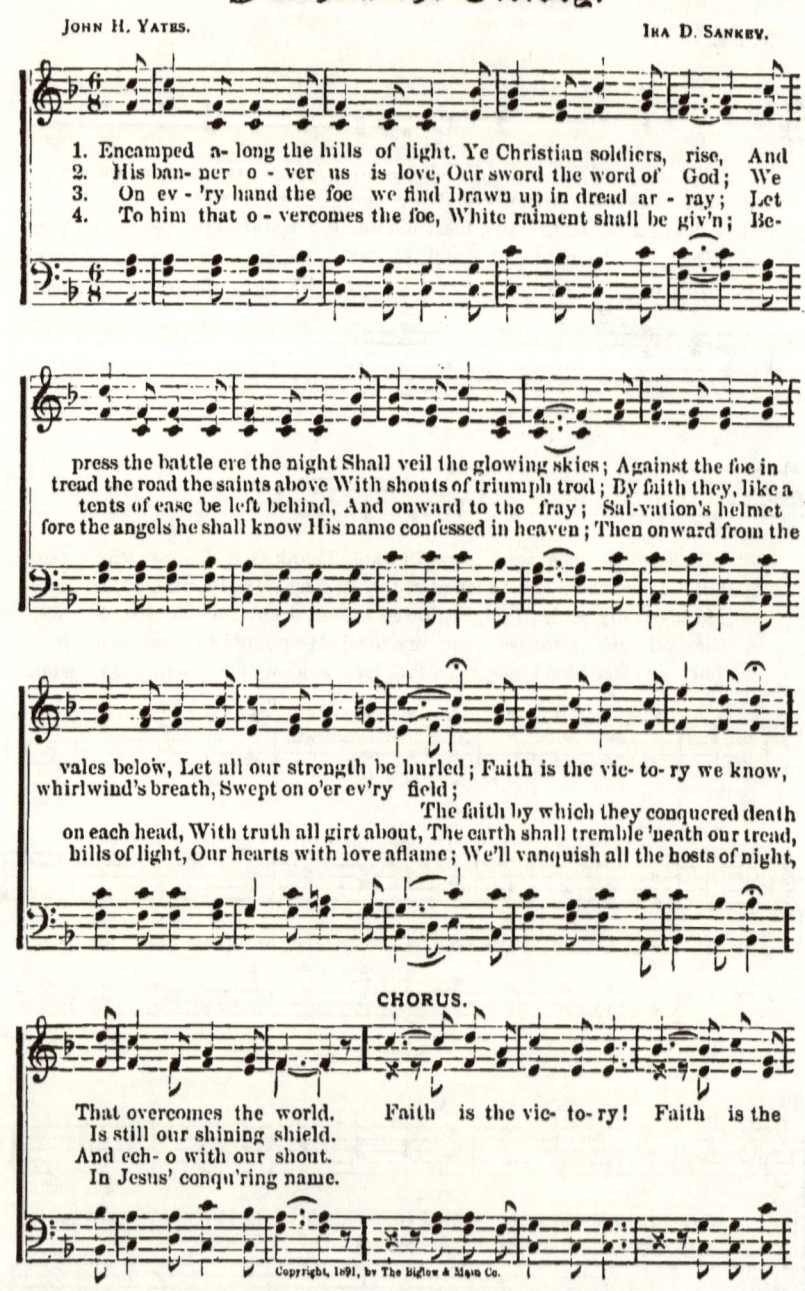

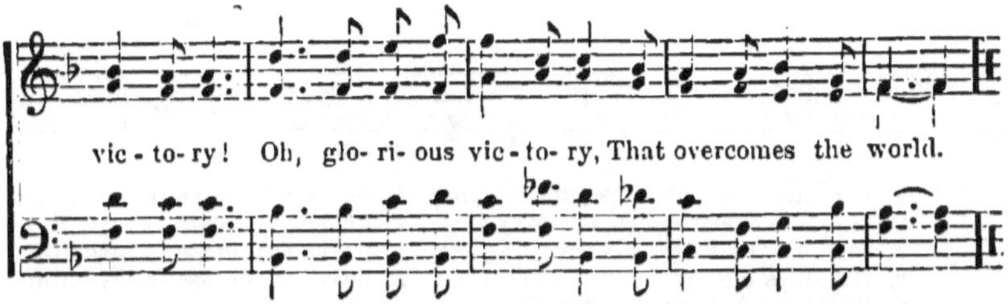

Faith is the Victory.—CONCLUDED. 21

vic-to-ry! Oh, glo-ri-ous vic-to-ry, That overcomes the world.

What a Meeting.

W. J. K.   W. J. KING.

1. What a meeting that will be in heaven, On that great day,
2. No more sorrows will a-wait our coming Where all is love;
3. Oh, what joy when we behold our mansions, All bright and fair,

When we greet again our friends and lov'd ones, With them to stay.
Sin and pain will nev-er more distress us In heav'n a-bove.
See the bless-ed face of our Redeem-er In glo-ry there.

CHORUS.

What a meet - - ing, When we raise the new, new song;
What a happy meeting, What a happy meeting,

Joining in ten thousand hal-le-lu-jahs With the blood wash'd throng.

Copyright, 1890, by Wm. J. Kirkpatrick.

Christ Within.

23

Rev. B. Carradine, D. D. Jno. R. Sweney.

1. My heart was once heavy with sadness And struggling with burdens and sin,
2. Once Jesus would visit his dwelling, Then leave thro' my doubt or my sin;
3. The grave was once dark to my vision, A goal that I cared not to win;
4. I oft-en repined un-der crosses, And knew not repining was sin;

But now it is thrilling with gladness, For Je-sus is dwelling with-in.
But now I rejoice in the tell-ing, My Saviour a-bideth with-in.
A gate now to countries e-ly-sian! Since Jesus is dwelling with-in.
I shout now o'er burdens and losses, For Je-sus is dwelling with-in.

CHORUS.

O glo-ry to God! the Saviour has come; He dwells in my heart and makes it his home: I hear his sweet voice and feel his own blood, And shout on my way, at home and abroad,—O glo - ry, glo-ry to God!

Copyright, 1894, by Jno. R. Sweney.

5 Gone now is the sighing and sorrow,
  The cares and the fears of the day;
  I ask not what comes with the morrow,
  For Jesus is in me to stay.

6 Let Satan and man now assail me,
  Let death lay me low in the grave;
  The Victor within will not fail me,
  What more can I pray for, or have?

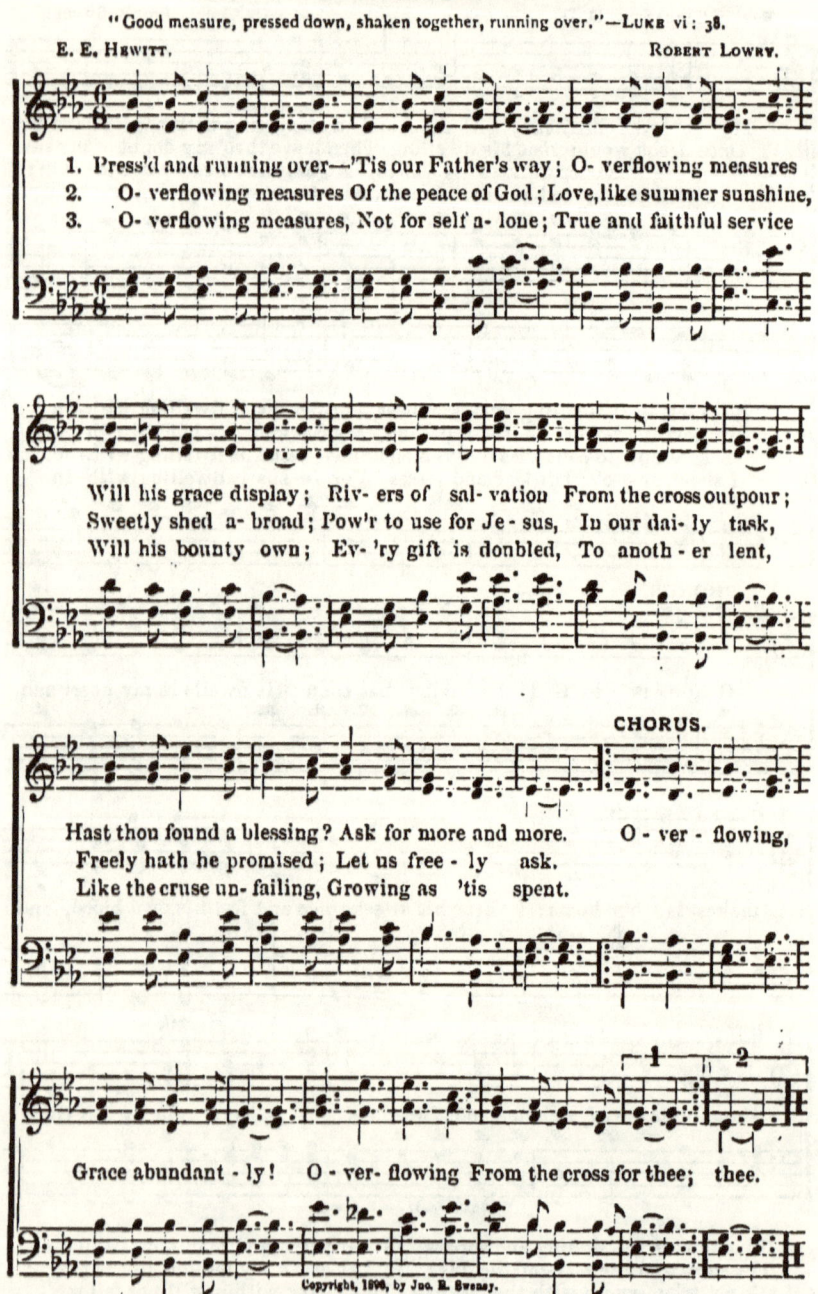

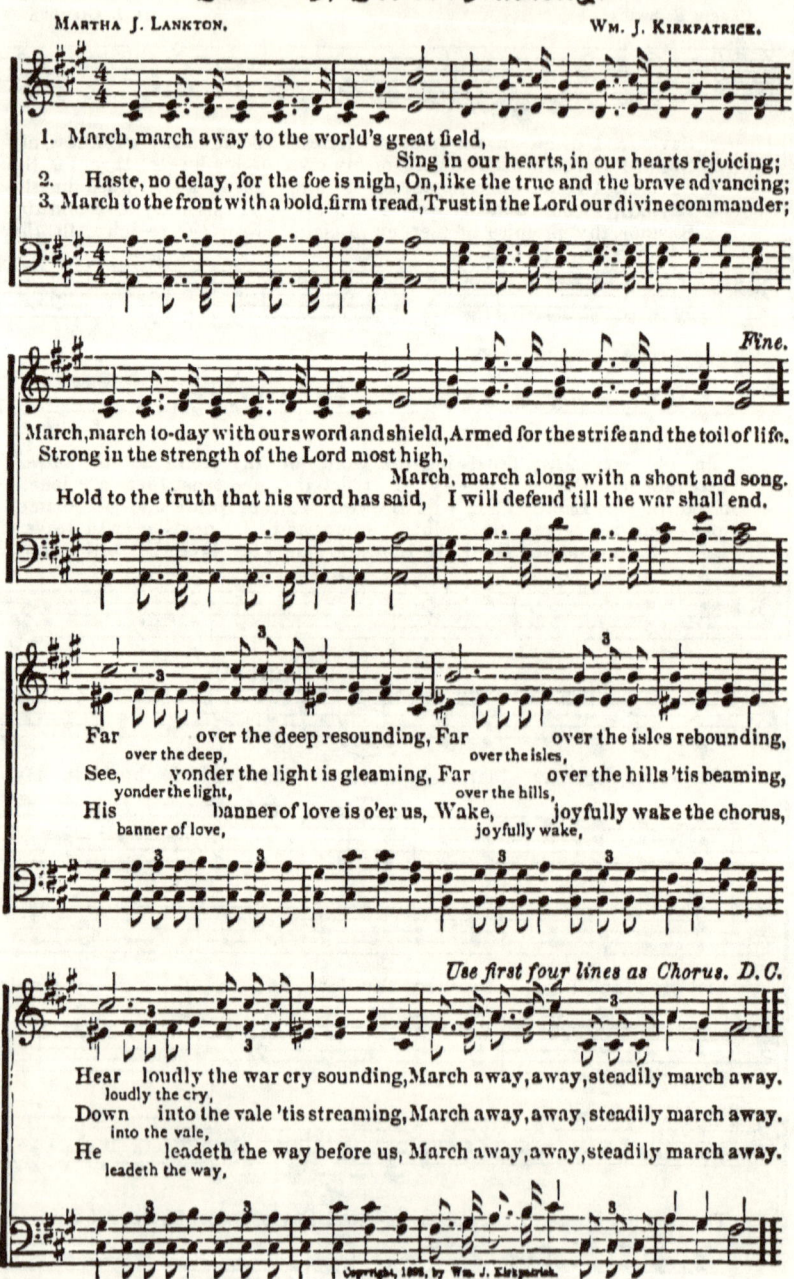

28. I Will Cling to the Rock of Ages.

JENNIE WILSON.   I. H. MEREDITH.

1. When life's billows beat and the tempest rages, There is still one refuge that standeth sure; I will close-ly cling to the Rock of A-ges, For I know that there I can rest se-cure.
2. To the Rock I'll cling when the skies are smiling, And the sunlit waves seek to lure a-way; When the world's vain joys are my soul beguiling, In that bless-ed place I will ev-er stay.
3. To the Rock I'll cling till the light eternal In its glory breaks on my wait-ing soul, And with an-gel voi-ces in songs su-pernal Still that safe re-treat I would fain ex-tol.

CHORUS.

I will cling, closely cling to the Rock of A-ges, In its sacred cleft can no harm betide; I will cling, ever cling to the Rock of A-ges, And by grace divine I will there a-bide.

Copyright, 1896, by John J. Hood.

It Just Suits Me.

E. E. Hewitt. Wm. J. Kirkpatrick.

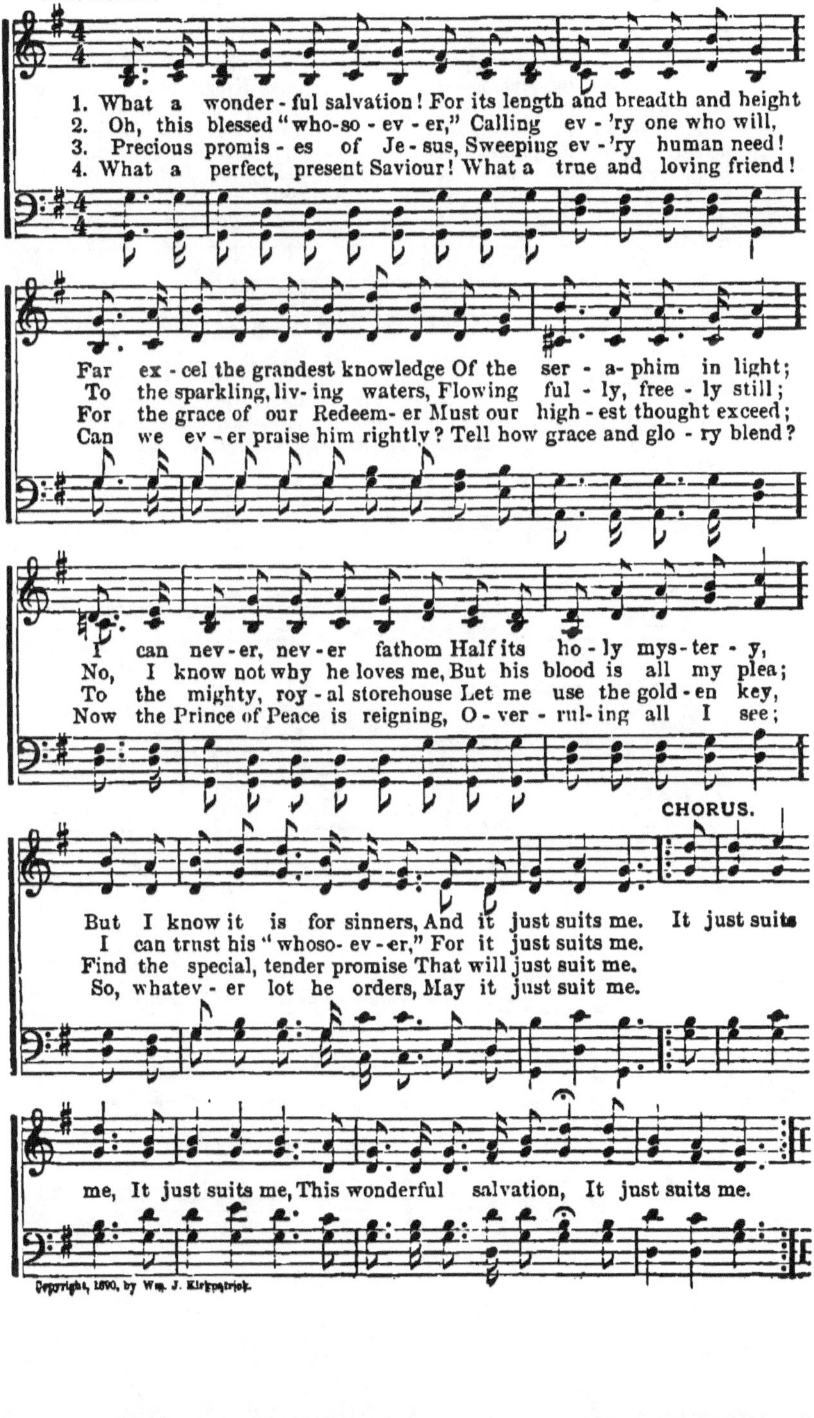

1. What a wonder-ful salvation! For its length and breadth and height
2. Oh, this blessed "who-so-ev-er," Calling ev-'ry one who will,
3. Precious promis-es of Je-sus, Sweeping ev-'ry human need!
4. What a perfect, present Saviour! What a true and loving friend!

Far ex-cel the grandest knowledge Of the ser-a-phim in light;
To the sparkling, liv-ing waters, Flowing ful-ly, free-ly still;
For the grace of our Redeem-er Must our high-est thought exceed;
Can we ev-er praise him rightly? Tell how grace and glo-ry blend?

I can nev-er, nev-er fathom Half its ho-ly mys-ter-y,
No, I know not why he loves me, But his blood is all my plea;
To the mighty, roy-al storehouse Let me use the gold-en key,
Now the Prince of Peace is reigning, O-ver-rul-ing all I see;

CHORUS.

But I know it is for sinners, And it just suits me. It just suits
I can trust his "whoso-ev-er," For it just suits me.
Find the special, tender promise That will just suit me.
So, whatev-er lot he orders, May it just suit me.

me, It just suits me, This wonderful salvation, It just suits me.

Copyright, 1890, by Wm. J. Kirkpatrick.

The Old Fountain.—CONCLUDED.

prophets and the sages Caught the singing of its waters, Long ago. Long ago.

4 As the eunuch tried to read
Philip taught him of his need,
And baptized him in the stream,
  Long ago;
As the outward seal and sign
Of an inward work divine,
That was wrought through that old [fountain,
  Long ago.

5 O thou fountain, deep and wide,
Flowing from the wounded side
That was pierced for our redemption,
  Long ago;
In thy ever-cleansing wave
There is found all pow'r to save,
'Tis the pow'r that heal'd the nations,
  Long ago.

Oh, Wondrous Rock!

"I will put thee in a cleft of the rock."—Ex. xxx: 22.

E. G.   EDWIN GARDNER.

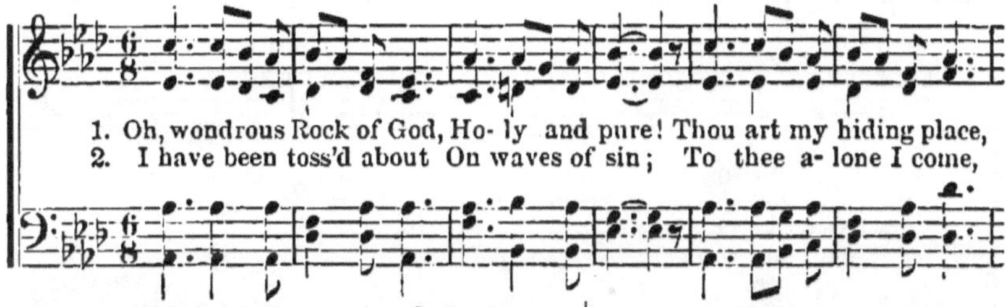

1. Oh, wondrous Rock of God, Ho-ly and pure! Thou art my hiding place,
2. I have been toss'd about On waves of sin; To thee a-lone I come,

From harm secure. Strong as eternal hills Thou shalt abide; There, in thy
Oh, let me in. There is no other place Where I would be So safe for

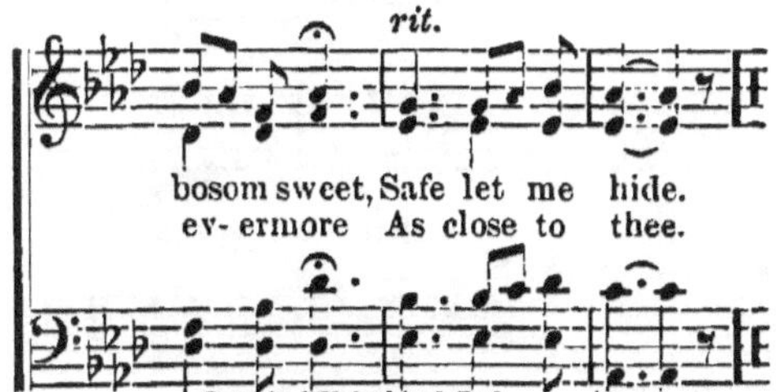

rit.

bosom sweet, Safe let me hide.
ev-ermore As close to thee.

3 To thee, my blessed Rock,
   My all I bring;
  In thee will I abide,
   And to thee cling.
  Safe where no ill can harm,
   Or dark wave roll,
  Within thy riven side,
   Oh, hide my soul.

Copyright, 1896, by John J. Hood.

5 I'll praise him with my dying breath,
  I'm wondrously saved to-day,
Who saved from Satan, sin and death,
  I'm wondrously saved to-day.

6 And then I'll praise him up in heav'n,
  I'm wondrously saved to-day, [giv'n,
Where blood-washed robes and harps are
  I'm wondrously saved to-day.

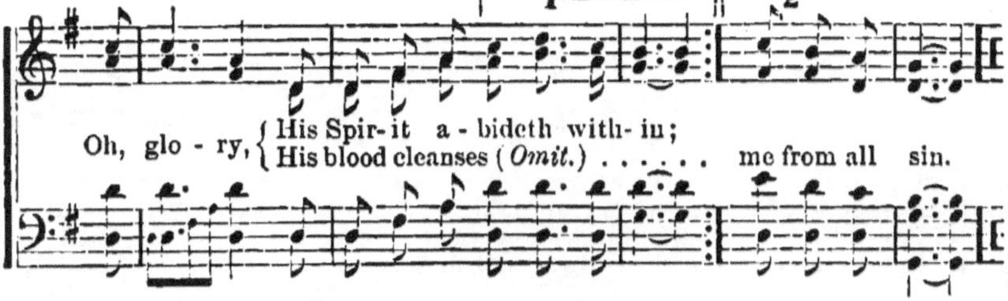

He Saves Me.—CONCLUDED.

Oh, glo-ry, { His Spir-it a-bideth with-in; His blood cleanses (*Omit.*) ...... me from all sin.

Under the Cross.

WM. MCDONALD.
E. O. EXCELL. By per.

1. I am coming to the cross, I am poor, and weak, and blind;
2. Long my heart has sigh'd for thee, Long has e-vil reign'd with-in;
3. Here I give my all to thee, Friends, and time, and earthly store;

I am counting all but dross, I shall full sal-va-tion find......
Je-sus sweetly speaks to me, "I will cleanse you from all sin."......
Soul and bod-y thine to be, Wholly thine for-ev-er-more......

Hal-le-lujah!

CHORUS.

Un-der the cross I lay my sins, Un-der the cross they lie;

Un-der the cross I lay my sins, Un-der the cross I'll die.

Copyright, 1889, by E. O. Excell.

In the Sunshine.—CONCLUDED.

In the sunshine, blessed sunshine, I am walking, I am walking in the light.
In the sunshine,

The Joy of Knowing Jesus.

ABBIE MILLS. H. L. GILMOUR.

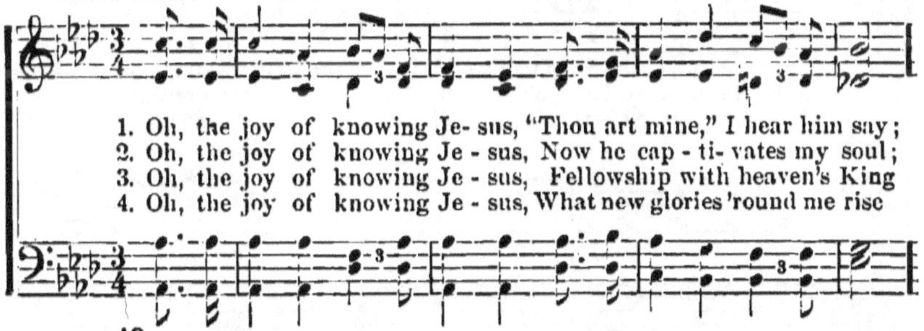

1. Oh, the joy of knowing Je-sus, "Thou art mine," I hear him say;
2. Oh, the joy of knowing Je-sus, Now he cap-ti-vates my soul;
3. Oh, the joy of knowing Je-sus, Fellowship with heaven's King
4. Oh, the joy of knowing Je-sus, What new glories 'round me rise

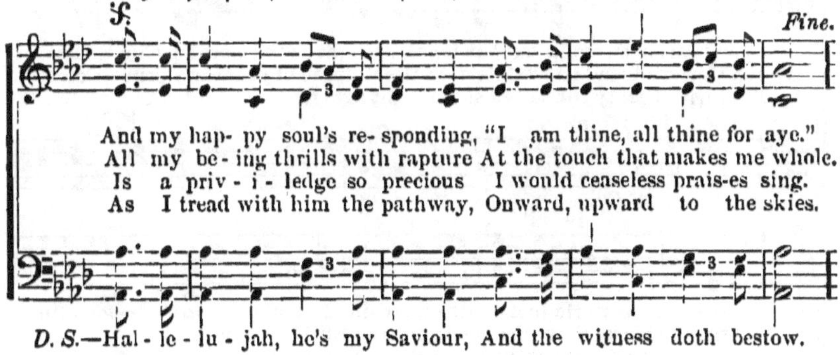

And my hap-py soul's re-sponding, "I am thine, all thine for aye."
All my be-ing thrills with rapture At the touch that makes me whole.
Is a priv-i-ledge so precious I would ceaseless prais-es sing.
As I tread with him the pathway, Onward, upward to the skies.

D. S.—Hal-le-lu-jah, he's my Saviour, And the witness doth bestow.

CHORUS.

Oh, the joy of knowing Je-sus, This my boast where'er I go;
Oh, the joy   This my boast

Copyright, 1894, by H. L. Gilmour.

5 Oh, the joy of knowing Jesus,
   Every wondrous promise mine,
   And by these I am partaken,
   Of the strength, and power divine.

6 Oh, the joy of knowing Jesus,
   When the fires around me glow,
   Then how intimate the glory;
   Thus, I more of Jesus know.

Sometime.—CONCLUDED. 47

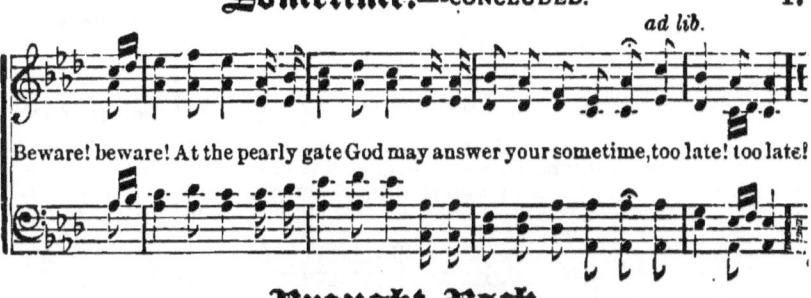

Beware! beware! At the pearly gate God may answer your sometime, too late! too late!

Brought Back.

H. L. Gilmour. Arr. by J. J. H.

1. How restless the soul of the wand'rer from Jesus! No spot in the wide world can
Unconscious he drifts on the waves of his folly, Still farther and farther a-
2. His soul in sad exile now longs for the homestead, And deep'ning convictions are
He hears as in childhood, those sweet words of Jesus, "Come, all ye that labor, and

D. C.—And chords of "sweet home," that have long been reposing,
By fingers unseen are a-
D. C. He ventures in weakness, but strength is imparted, And gladly he's welcomed by

comfort afford. ⎱ Yet still there are moments of fond recollection,
way from his Lord. ⎰ When bright scenes of
tossing his breast. ⎱ He listens! the Spirit repeats the sweet message,
I'll give you rest. ⎰ And turning from

wakened anew.
Father at home.

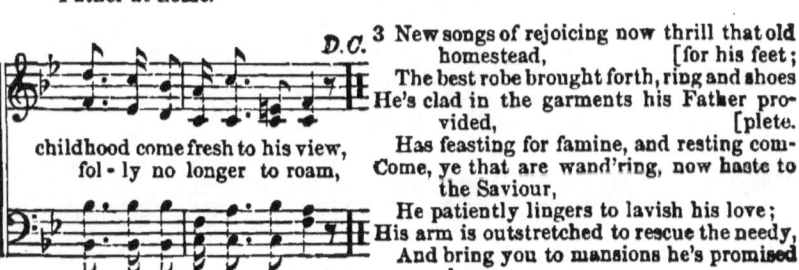

childhood come fresh to his view,
fol - ly no longer to roam,

3 New songs of rejoicing now thrill that old
 homestead, [for his feet;
The best robe brought forth, ring and shoes
He's clad in the garments his Father pro-
 vided, [plete.
Has feasting for famine, and resting com-
Come, ye that are wand'ring, now haste to
 the Saviour,
He patiently lingers to lavish his love;
His arm is outstretched to rescue the needy,
And bring you to mansions he's promised
 above.

Copyright, 1891, by H. L. Gilmour.

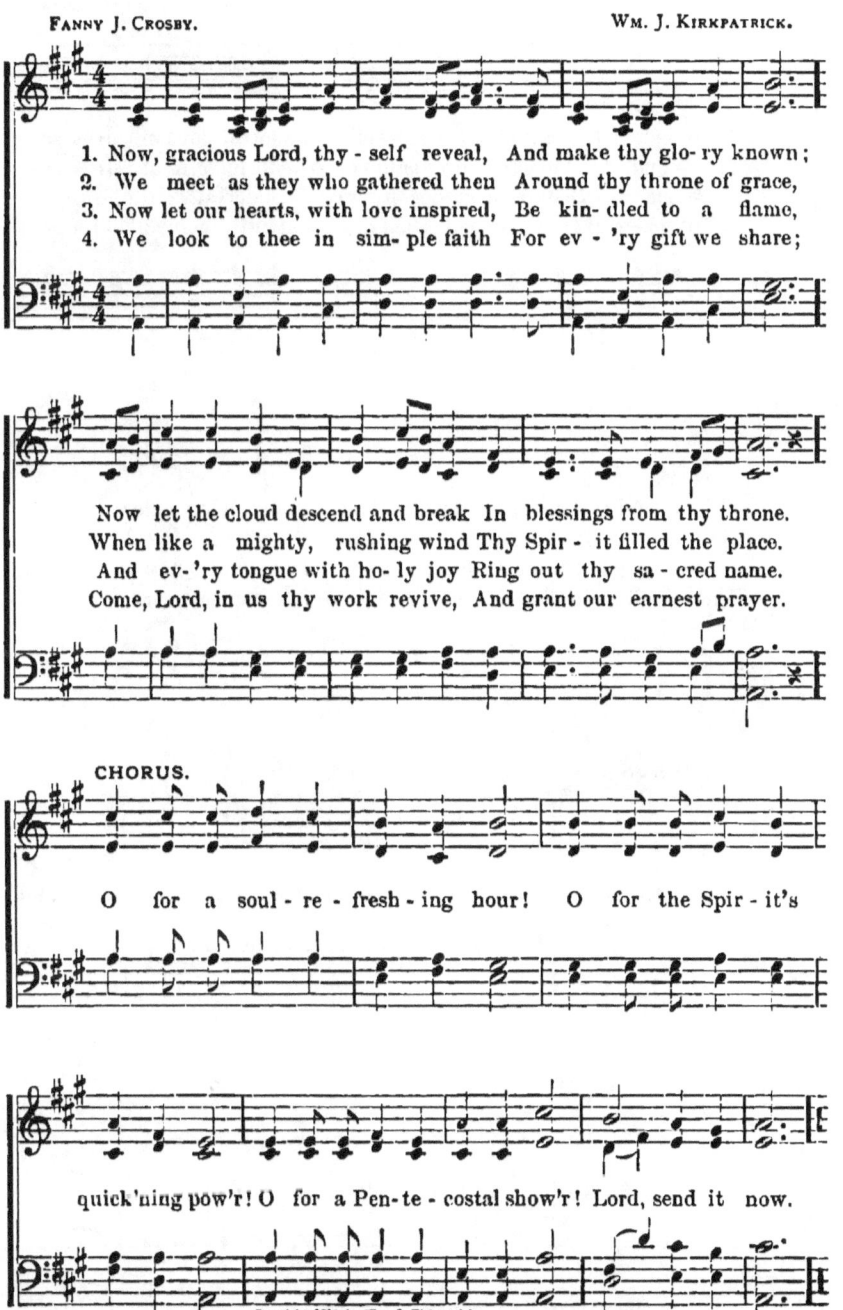

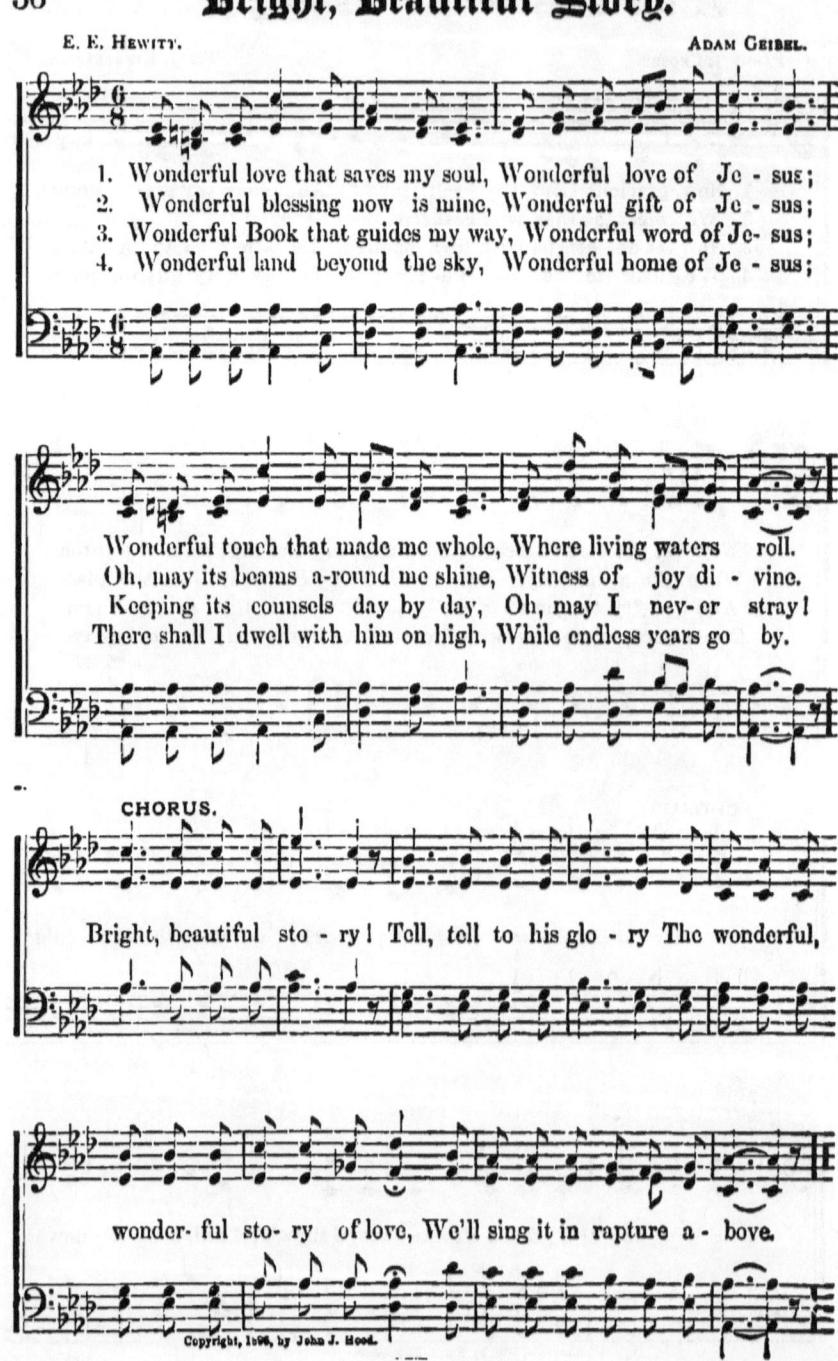

5 Go, sit with the mighty in purple and gold, [untold;
Thy mansions be stately, thy treasures
But soon thou shalt dwell in the damp house of clay, [selves and away.
While thy riches make wings to them-

6 Oh, give me the riches that fade not nor fly,
A treasure up yonder, a home in the sky;
Where beautiful things in their beauty still stay, [ed away.
And where riches ne'er fly from the bless-

There is a Refuge.

Ida L. Reed.
W. T. Dashiell.

1. There is a ref- - - uge sweet, secure,
2. When danger threat- - - ens, thou canst fly
3. There is a ref- - - uge, peaceful, calm,

For ev'ry bur- - - dened soul, In Jesus' love . . . it standeth sure, .
Unto this strong- - - hold free; When unto him . . thy soul shall cry, .
In Jesus' love . . 'tis found, And there each heart . shall find a balm .

Tho' heavy tem- - - pests roll Across the breast, . they can not harm, .
He'll help and com- - - fort thee. He'll keep thee safe . within his hand, .
For ev'ry bleed- - - ing wound. For ev'ry bur- - - - den, ev'ry pain, .

If thou to him . . . wilt go, . . Protected by . . .
And nev-er let . . . thee go; . . Firm by his grace . .
There waits a sweet . . . re-lease, And thou with him . . .

his mighty arm, ... Full safe-ty thou shalt know.
thy feet shall stand, . . . Joy-springs for thee shall flow.
in heav'n shall reign, . . . In ev-er-last-ing peace.

Copyright, 1896, by Jno. R. Sweney.

The Sweet Beulah Land.

"Let us go up at once and possess it;" Nu. xiii: 30.

Rev. H. J. Zelley. H. L. Gilmour.

1. I am walking to-day in the sweet Beu-lah land, I have
2. I am now go-ing on to explore Beu-lah land, 'Tis the
3. I have found a sweet peace that the world can-not know, As I
4. Oh, the sweetness of love that en-raptures my soul, For com-

crossed to the glo-ry side, I am washed in the blood, and my
gift of my Lord to me; I am tasting its joys, I am
walk by my Saviour's side, I am kept by his power, I am
mun-ion with Christ I know! I am hap-py in him, and to-

soul is made white, And I know I am sanc-ti-fied.
walking in light, And the face of my Saviour see.
led by his hand, And I'll ev-er with him a-bide.
day thro' my soul Living streams of sal-va-tion flow.

CHORUS.

Glo-ry, Glory to God, oh, Glo-ry to God, My heart is now cleansed from sin, from sin, I've abandoned my-self to the Ho-ly Ghost, And his ful-ness a-bides with-in.

Copyright, 1891, by H. L. Gilmour.

Love and Praise — 5

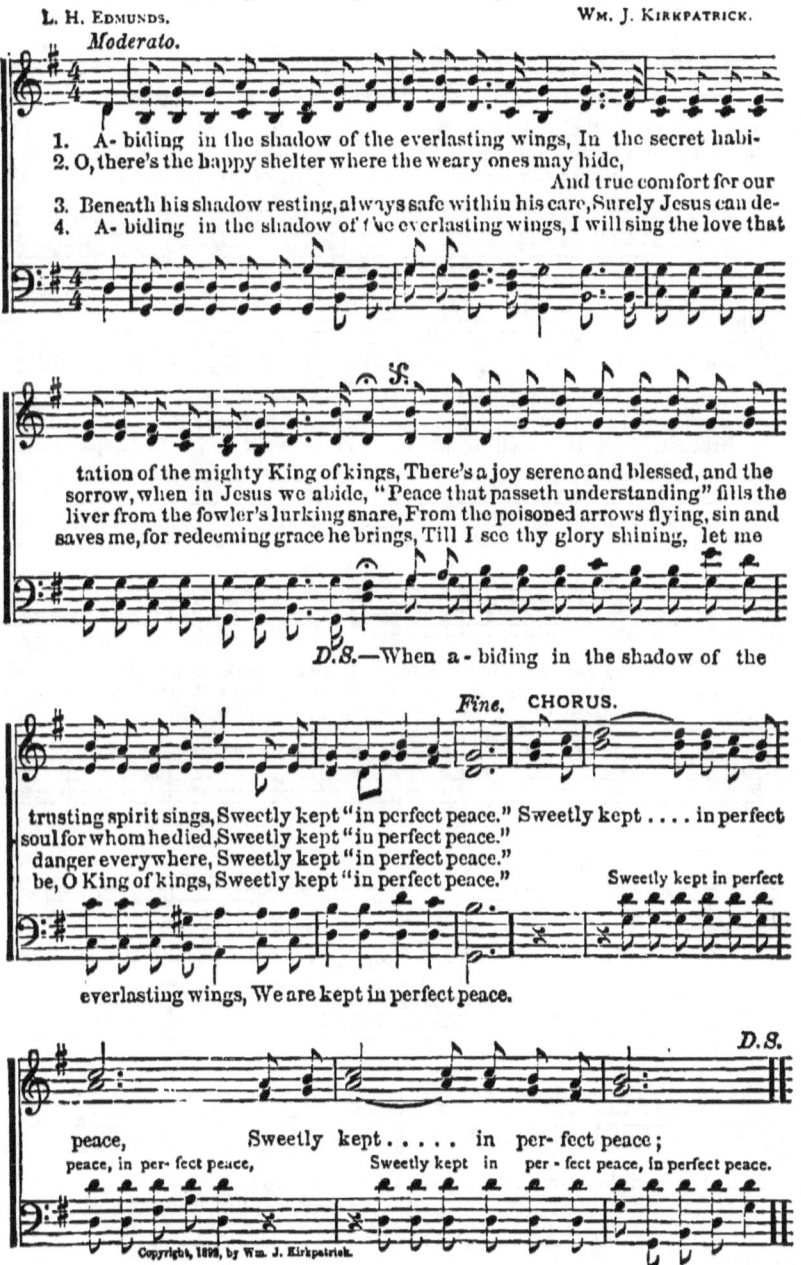

5 Calm 'midst the waves of trouble be,
   He's just the same Jesus
   As when he hushed the raging sea,
   The very same Jesus.

6 Some day our raptured eyes shall see
   He's just the same Jesus;
   Oh, blessed day for you and me!
   The very same Jesus.

72. Gladly We Will Go.

FANNY J. CROSBY.   CLARISSA H. SPENCER.

1. The Lord is our shepherd, precious friend and guide, We'll trust him ever,
trust him ev-er, walking by his side; Be this our en-dea-vor faithful-
ly to show, Where Jesus leads our willing feet beside him still shall go.

2. Thro' sunshine or tempest, o-ver land or sea, Whate'er befalls us,
where he calls us, quickly we would be; The toils that a-wait us tho' we
cannot know, At his command with heart and hand beside him we will go.

3. The Lord is our keep-er, watching ev-er near, In him confid-ing,
firm abiding, wherefore should we fear? We'll cling to the promise left us
here be-low, And wheresoe'er he leadeth us beside him we will go.

CHORUS.

We'll go, we'll go, we'll glad-ly, glad-ly go, Tho' skies are
dark and chill-y winds may blow; The lost to find, or

Copyright, 1895, by Wm. J. Kirkpatrick.

Gladly We Will Go.—CONCLUDED.

bravely meet the foe, Wherever Jesus calls us we'll gladly, gladly go.

Prevailing Prayer.

"For as a prince hast thou power with God, and with men, and hast prevailed."

Mrs. E. E. WILLIAMS.   H. L. GILMOUR.

1. Come, Holy Ghost, thy temple claim, And now therein set up thy throne;
2. The carnal mind within me slay, From inbred sin, oh, set me free;
3. Thy nature, Lord, to me impart, Thy boundless grace and mercy prove;

With fires of love my soul inflame, And make and seal me all thine own.
Hear thou my cry, turn not away, But come and live thy life in me.
Make me this moment pure in heart, And fill me with thy perfect love.

D.S.—The blood! the blood! the precious blood! It cleanseth me, it cleanseth me.

CHORUS.

I can believe! I do believe! My pray'r prevails! my soul is free!

Copyright, 1896, by H. L. Gilmour.

4 'Tis done! the gracious work divine!
  My fervent prayer prevails with God;
  Pardon and purity are mine,
  Thro' faith in Christ's atoning blood.

5 Now, O my soul, his praises sing,
  And to the world his love proclaim;
  Your trophies to his footstool bring,
  And shout hosanna to his name.

I've Heard of a Saviour.—CONCLUDED.

CHORUS.

My sins rose as high as a mountain, They all disappeared in the Fountain; He put my name down for a palace and crown, O bless his dear name, I am free.

The Heaven-bound Mariner.

Words arranged.
Arr. by Wm. J. Kirkpatrick.

1. What ves-sel are you sailing in? Pray tell to me its name. Our ves-sel is the Ark of God, And Christ our Captain's name.
2. And what's the port your sailing to? Declare to me straight way. The new Je-ru-salem's the Port, In realms of end-less day.
3. Our compass is the Sacred Word, Our anchor, blooming Hope, The love of God the main top-sail, And faith our ca-ble rope.
4. And are you not afraid some storm Your bark will o-verwhelm? We do not fear, the Lord is here, Our Fath-er's at the helm.

Cho. { Then hoist your sail to catch the gale, Each sail-or ply his oar, The
     { We soon shall reach the shore, We soon shall reach the shore, The

night be-gins to wear a-way, We soon shall reach the shore.

From "Songs of Joy and Gladness."

5 Heave out your boat, I too will go,
    If you can find me room.
   There's room for you, and all who will,
    Make no delay to come.   [storm

6 We've looked astern, through many a
    The Lord has brought us through;
   We're looking now ahead, and lo!
    The land appears in view.

7 The sun is up, the clouds are gone,
    The heavens above are clear,
   A city bright appears in sight,
    We soon shall round the pier.

8 And when we all are landed safe,
    On that celestial plain,
   Our song shall be "Worthy the Lamb
    That was for sinners slain."

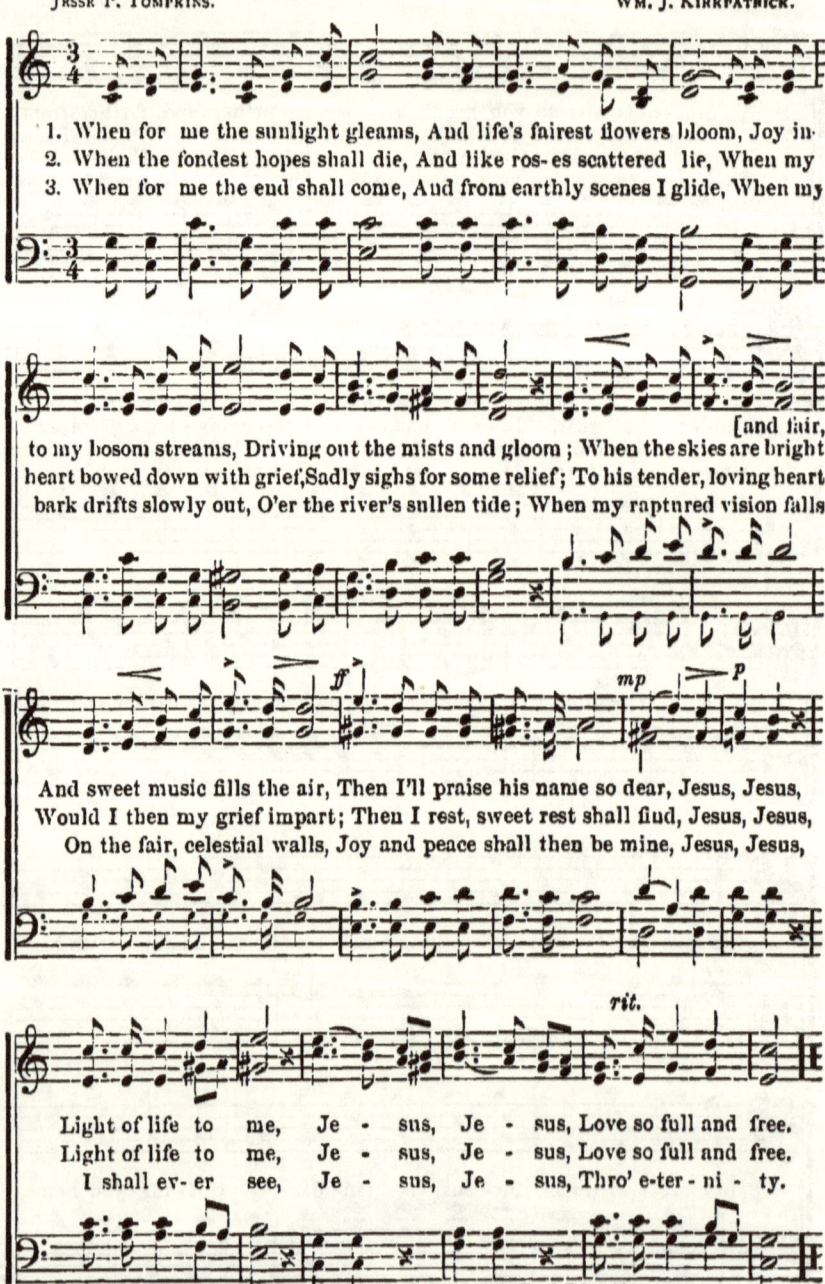

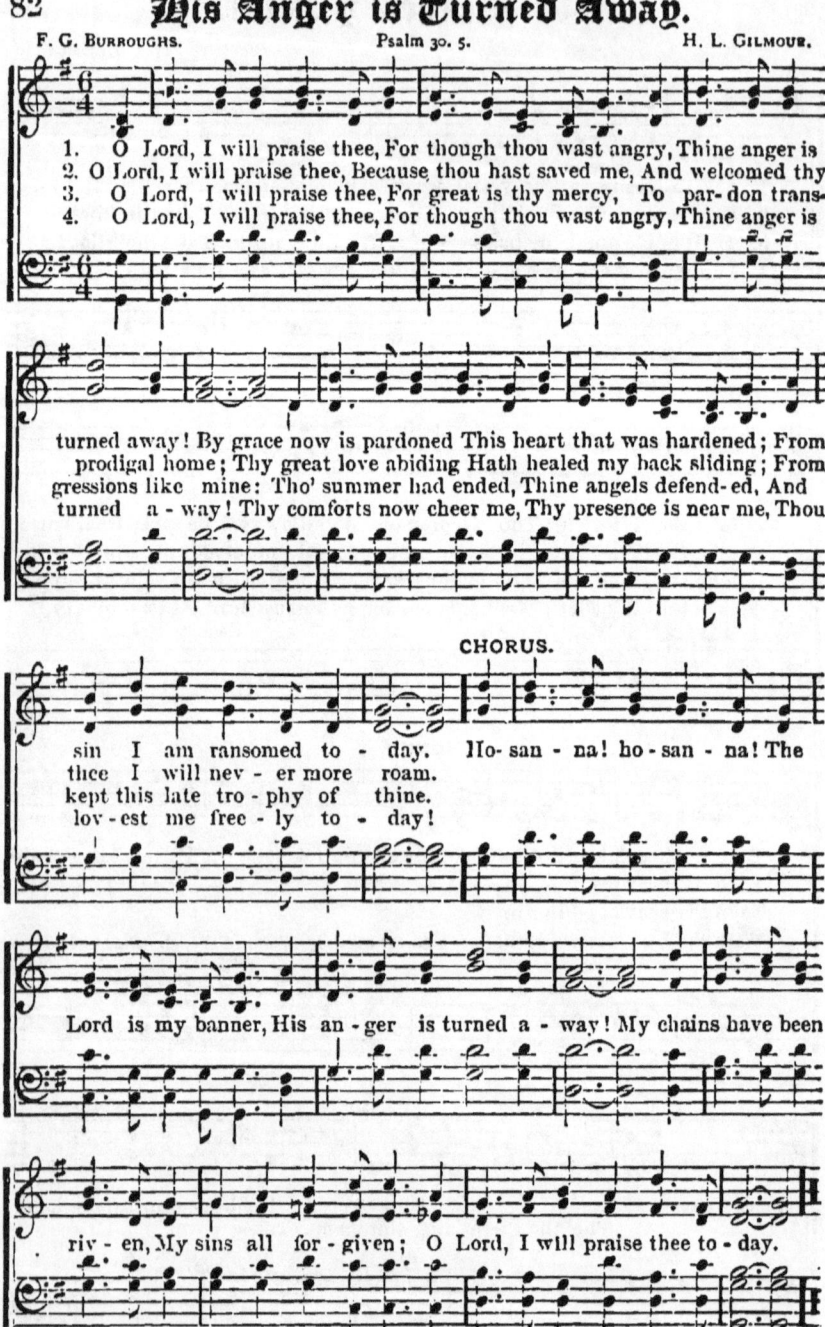

Just Lean upon Jesus.

E. E. Hewitt. Wm. J. Kirkpatrick.

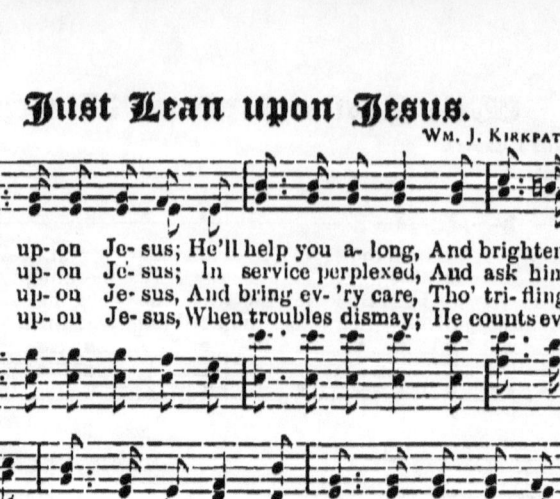

1. Just lean up-on Je-sus; He'll help you a-long, And brighten your
2. Just lean up-on Je-sus; In service perplexed, And ask him to
3. Just lean up-on Je-sus, And bring ev-'ry care, Tho' tri-fling or
4. Just lean up-on Je-sus, When troubles dismay; He counts ev-'ry

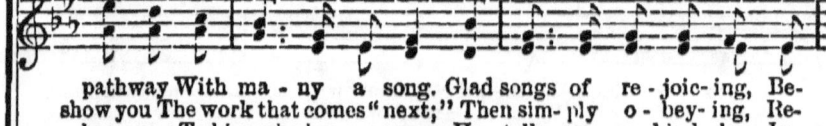

pathway With ma-ny a song. Glad songs of re-joic-ing, Be-
show you The work that comes "next;" Then sim-ply o-bey-ing, Re-
heav-y, To him who hears prayer. He tells you so kind-ly In
footstep That leads up to Day. So near "the Be-lov-ed" No

cause he is near, So might-y to save you, So will-ing to cheer.
sults leave with him; His arm is un-fail-ing, His eye nev-er dim.
him to con-fide, Oh, trust him most ful-ly, There's joy at his side.
ill need af-fright; The val-ley of shadow His presence makes bright.

CHORUS.

Just lean . . . up-on Je - - sus, Dear child . . of his care; . . . .
Just lean up-on Je-sus, just lean upon Je-sus, Just lean upon Jesus, Dear child of his care;

Just lean . . . up-on Je - - sus, Your bur-den he'll share. . . .
Just lean up-on Je-sus, Just lean upon Jesus, Your burden he'll share, Your burden he'll share.

Copyright, 1894, by Wm. J. Kirkpatrick.

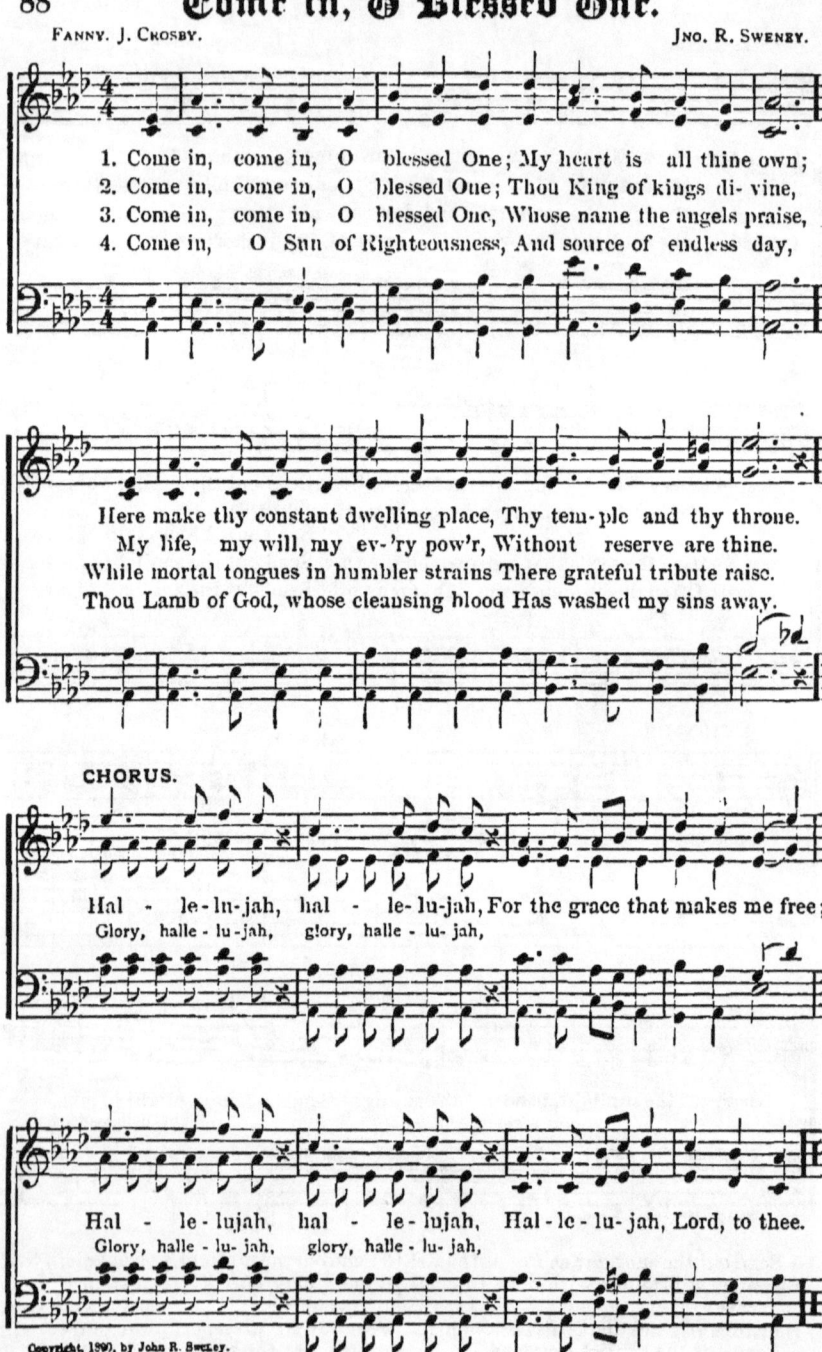

Make Me a Blessing To-day.

"Lord bless me, and make me a blessing."—Rev. D. B. Updegraff.

Rev. H. J. Zelley.   H. L. Gilmour.

1. I do not ask to choose my path, Lord, lead me in thy way;
2. Around me, Lord, are sin-ful men, Who scorn and dis-o-bey;
3. To those who once thy love have known, But now are far a-stray;
4. Some saints of thine are in distress, And for thy ful-ness pray;
5. If thou hast an-y errand, Lord, Send me, and I'll o-bey;

Inspire each thought and prompt each word, And make me a blessing to-day.
Use me to win them from their sins, And make me a blessing to-day.
Help me to lead them back to thee, And make me a blessing to-day.
Oh, let me go and help them Lord, And make me a blessing to-day.
Use me in an-y way thou wilt, And make me a blessing to-day.

CHORUS.

Bless me, Lord, and make me a blessing, I'll gladly thy message convey;
Use me to help some poor, needy soul, And make me a blessing to-day.

Copyright, 1894, by H. L. Gilmour.

'Tis Everything to Me.

(In answer to the hymn, "Is it Nothing to You?")

E. E. Hewitt.
Jno. R. Sweney.

1. The love of God to sinners, his "ev-er-lasting love," 'Tis everything to
2. The grace that never fails me, "sufficient" every day, 'Tis everything to
3. To know that I may serve him, his fellow-worker here, 'Tis everything to
4. To know I have a mansion prepared for me on high, 'Tis everything to

me, yes, everything to me; It brought the Lord my Saviour from radiant realms a-
me, yes, everything to me; A song in nights of sorrow, a star to guide my
me, yes, everything to me; To go up-on his errands, to tell his words of
me, yes, everything to me; That there I'll be with Jesus, beyond the sunset

D. S.—'round this blessed Saviour my best affections

Fine. CHORUS.

bove, 'Tis everything to me, yes, everything to me. 'Tis joy, 'tis joy to
way, 'Tis everything to me, yes, everything to me.
cheer, 'Tis everything to me, yes, everything to me.
sky, 'Tis everything to me, yes, everything to me.

twine, He's everything to me, yes, everything to me.

D. S.

know that he is mine, Since
That rays of heav'nly glory on my earthly path will shine;

Copyright, 1896, by Jno. R. Sweney.

Is it Nothing to You? 91

Suggested on hearing the sermon by Rev. B. Fay Mills, from the text, "Is it nothing to you?"
La. i: 12, preached at the Ocean Grove Auditorium, Aug. 24, 1894.

Myron W. Morse, and Fanny J. Crosby.　　　　　　　　Jno. R. Sweney.

1. Our blessed Redeemer is passing this way, Is it nothing to you, is it
2. The Master is calling, oh, list to his voice, Is it nothing to you, is it
3. You region so lovely, where all will be song, Is it nothing to you, is it

nothing to you? Oh, hear him this moment so ten-der-ly say, Is it
nothing to you? Awake from your slumber, believe and rejoice, Is it
nothing to you? The Saviour's glad welcome, the glorified throng, Are they

nothing, is it nothing to you? There is life for a look at the
nothing, is it nothing to you? The sands of your life are fast
nothing, are they nothing to you? The an- gels are there, brother,

cru - ci- fied One, There is life for a look at the Father's own Son; Oh,
pass- ing a- way, Oh, haste, quickly haste, ere the close of the day, Re-
where will you be?— 'Tis time that you halted on life's restless sea, And

hasten just now, to the dear Saviour come, Is it nothing, is it nothing to you?
pent and receive him, oh, do not delay, Make it something, make it something to you.
settled this question: "Did Christ die for me?" Is it nothing, is it nothing to you?

Copyright, 1894, by Jno. R. Sweney.

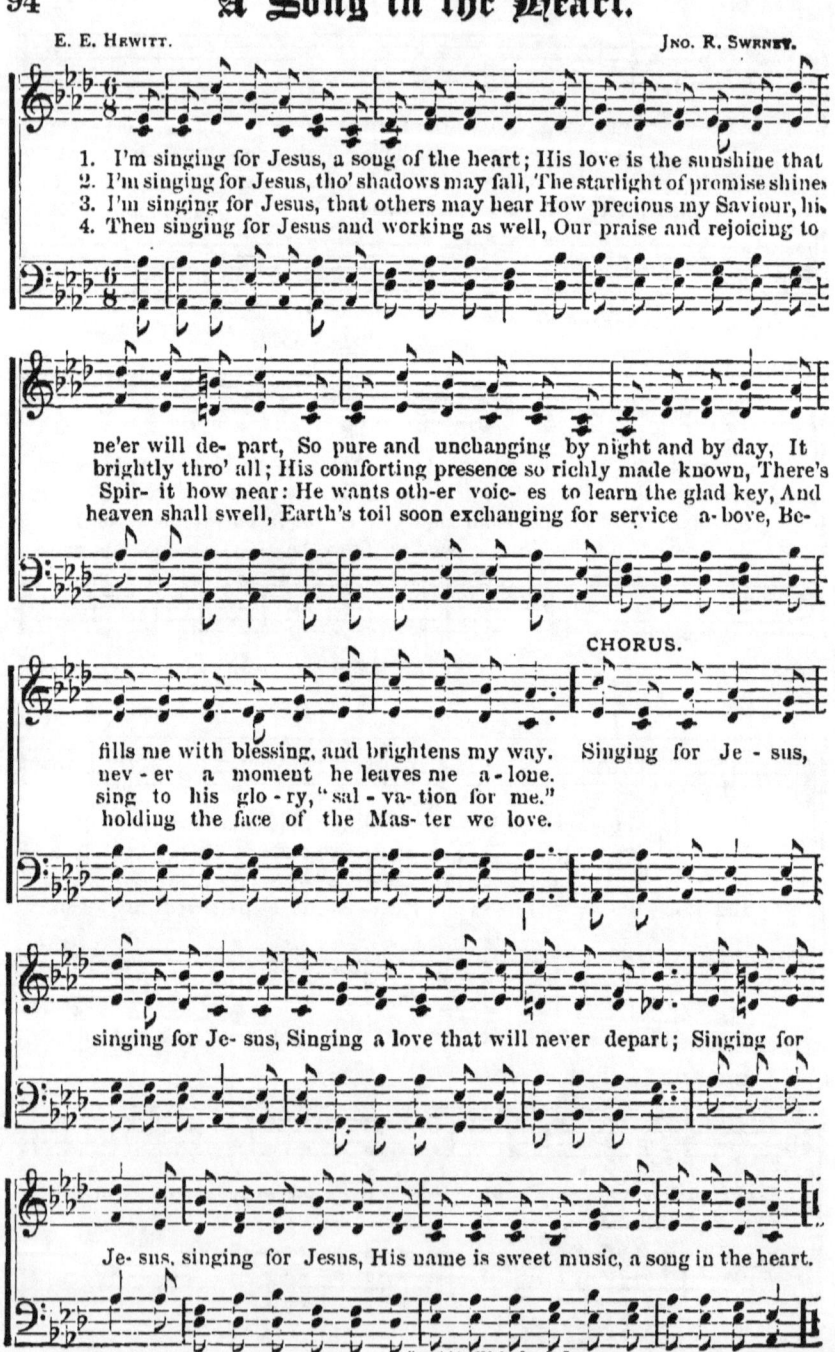

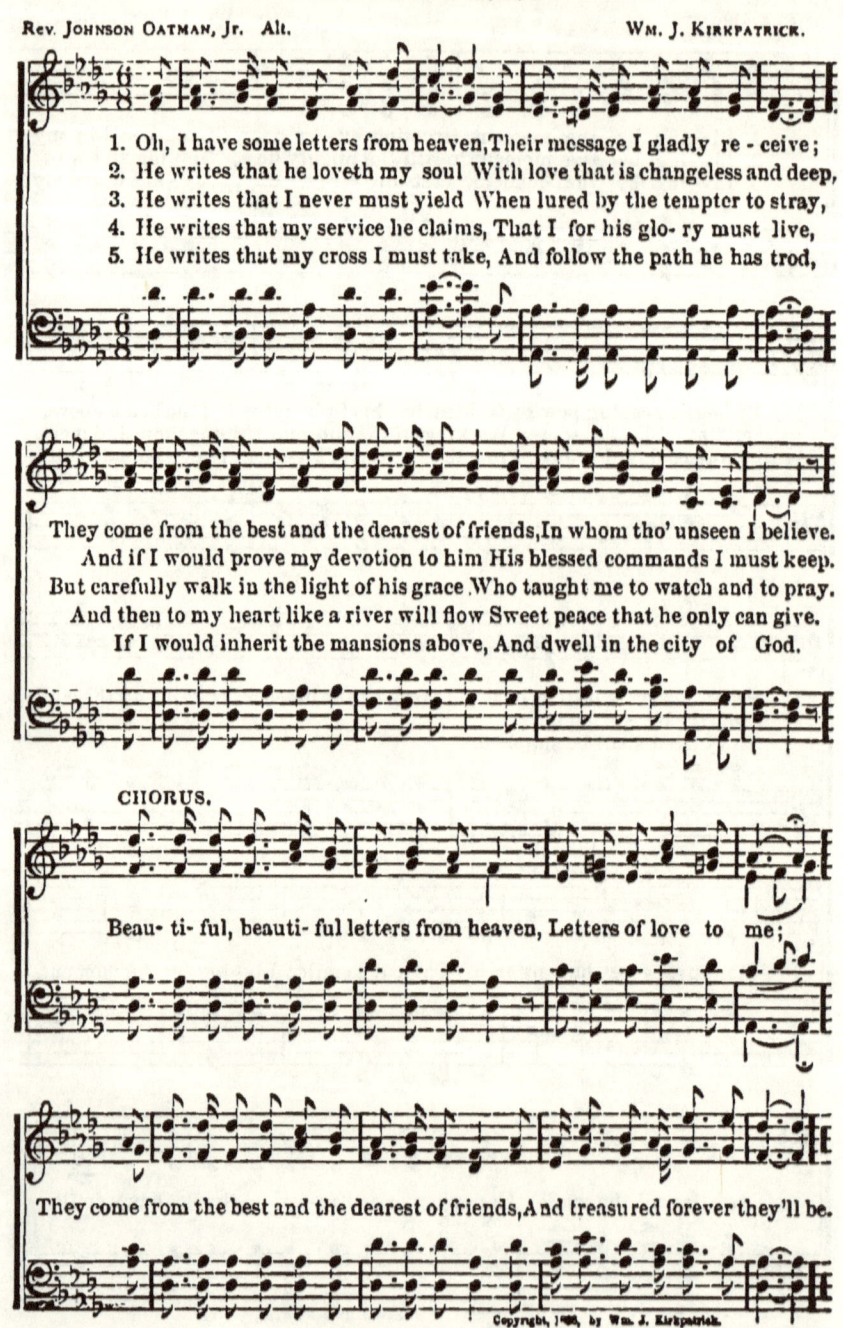

He Left the Ninety and Nine.

Rev. Johnson Oatman. Op. 99. H. L Gilmour.

1. The sheep were sleeping within the fold, The Shepherd counted the line, The night was dark, and the wind was cold, He counted ninety and nine; But one was lost on the mountain track, The Shepherd started to bring him back, And little knew of their Shepherd's pain, Who suffering thus one sheep to gain, Had heaven and earth took up the cry, " To save one sheep that was doomed to die, Christ left the ninety and nine. He left the ninety and nine, He left the ninety and nine;

2. Securely sheltered within the fold Remained the ninety and nine, Enjoying the Shepherd's wealth untold, Those happy ninety and nine; They

3. But at last went up a joyful cry, I've found this lost one of mine; He'll live with me in a home on high, Safe with the ninety and nine. Then

D. S.—How great was the cost, for the one that was lost, He left the ninety and nine.

Copyright, 1896, by H. L. Gilmour.

Tell it Out with Gladness.—CONCLUDED. 101

feel, Tell it out, tell it out with glad-ness.
world the joy you feel,

Lord, I'm Coming Home.

W. J. K.
With great feeling.
WM. J. KIRKPATRICK.

1. I've wandered far a-way from God, Now I'm coming home;
2. I've wast-ed ma-ny pre-cious years, Now I'm coming home;
3. I'm tired of sin and stray-ing, Lord, Now I'm coming home;
4. My soul is sick, my heart is sore, Now I'm coming home;

The paths of sin too long I've trod, Lord, I'm coming home.
I now re-pent with bit-ter tears, Lord, I'm coming home.
I'll trust thy love, be-lieve thy word, Lord, I'm coming home.
My strength renew, my hope re-store, Lord, I'm coming home.

D.S.—O-pen wide thine arms of love, Lord, I'm coming home.

CHORUS.

Coming home, coming home, Nev-er more to roam;

Copyright, 1892, by Wm. J. Kirkpatrick.

5 My only hope, my only plea,
  Now I'm coming home,
  That Jesus died, and died for me,
  Lord, I'm coming home.

6 I need his cleansing blood I know,
  Now I'm coming home;
  Oh, wash me whiter than the snow,
  Lord, I'm coming home.

Building Day by Day.—CONCLUDED.

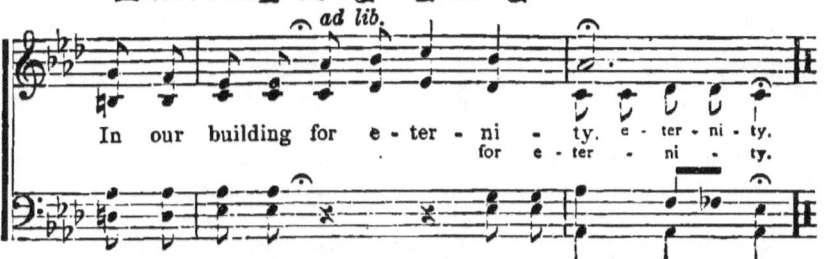

In our building for e-ter-ni-ty. e-ter-ni-ty.
for e-ter-ni-ty.

Wash Me, O Lamb of God.

H. B. BEEGLE. Wm. J. KIRKPATRICK.

May be used as a Duett.

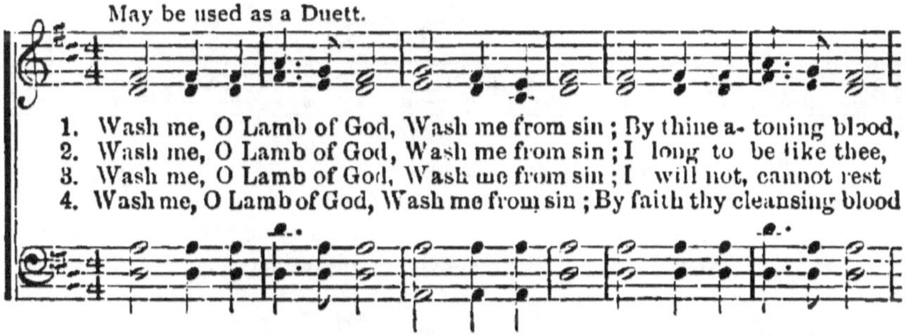

1. Wash me, O Lamb of God, Wash me from sin; By thine a- toning blood,
2. Wash me, O Lamb of God, Wash me from sin; I long to be like thee,
3. Wash me, O Lamb of God, Wash me from sin; I will not, cannot rest
4. Wash me, O Lamb of God, Wash me from sin; By faith thy cleansing blood

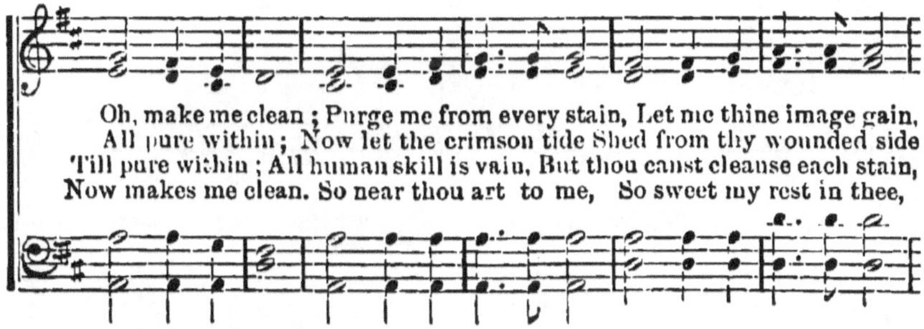

Oh, make me clean; Purge me from every stain, Let me thine image gain,
All pure within; Now let the crimson tide Shed from thy wounded side
Till pure within; All human skill is vain, But thou canst cleanse each stain,
Now makes me clean. So near thou art to me, So sweet my rest in thee,

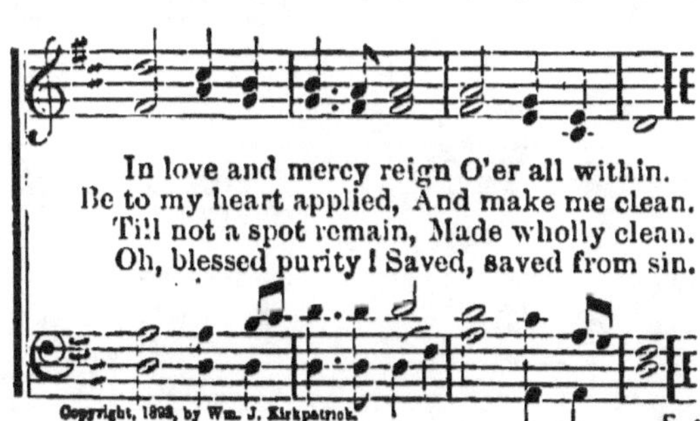

In love and mercy reign O'er all within.
Be to my heart applied, And make me clean.
Till not a spot remain, Made wholly clean.
Oh, blessed purity! Saved, saved from sin.

5 Wash me, O Lamb of God,
  Wash me from sin;
Thou, while I trust in thee,
  Wilt keep me clean;
Each day to thee I bring
Heart, life, yea, everything;
Saved while to thee I cling,
  Saved from all sin.

Copyright, 1898, by Wm. J. Kirkpatrick.

S. of Love and Praise, 3—K

106. There's a Hill Lone and Gray.

Rev. B. Carradine, D. D.   Jno. R. Sweney.

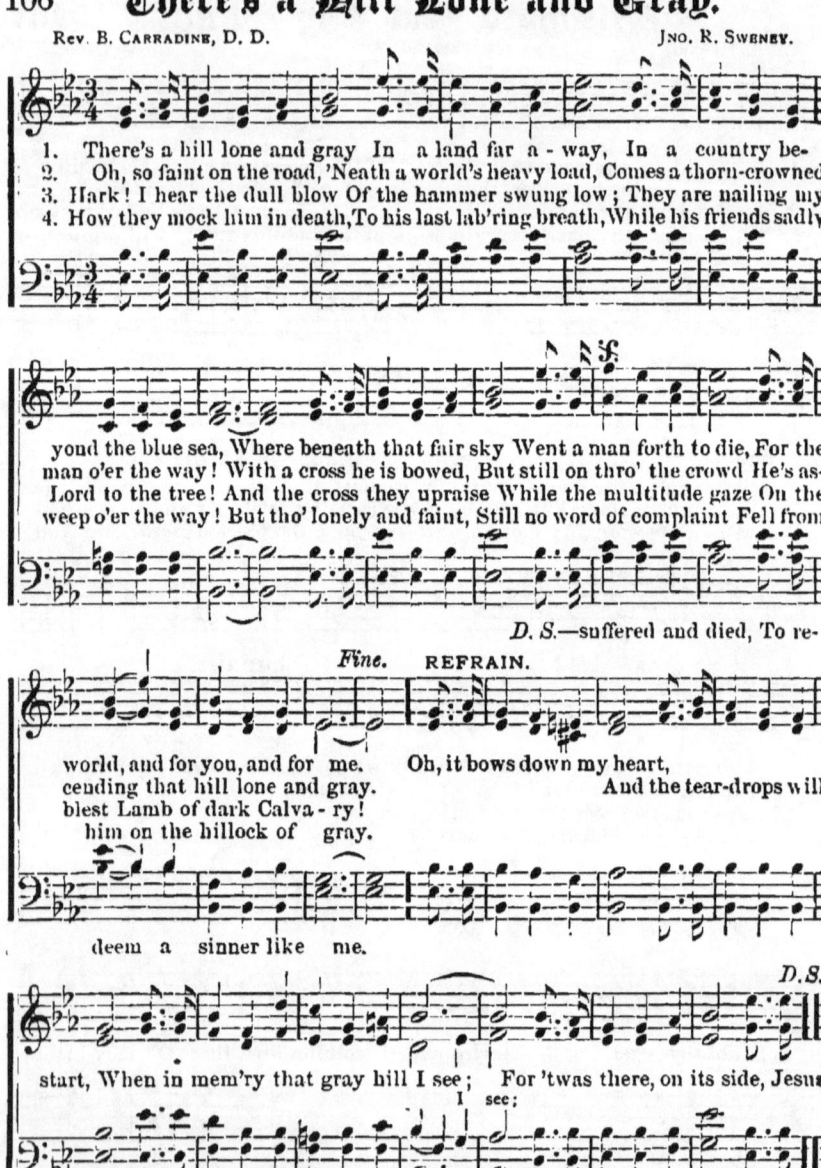

1. There's a hill lone and gray In a land far a-way, In a country beyond the blue sea, Where beneath that fair sky Went a man forth to die, For the world, and for you, and for me.
2. Oh, so faint on the road, 'Neath a world's heavy load, Comes a thorn-crowned man o'er the way! With a cross he is bowed, But still on thro' the crowd He's ascending that hill lone and gray.
3. Hark! I hear the dull blow Of the hammer swung low; They are nailing my Lord to the tree! And the cross they upraise While the multitude gaze On the blest Lamb of dark Calva-ry!
4. How they mock him in death, To his last lab'ring breath, While his friends sadly weep o'er the way! But tho' lonely and faint, Still no word of complaint Fell from him on the hillock of gray.

REFRAIN.

Oh, it bows down my heart, And the tear-drops will start, When in mem'ry that gray hill I see; For 'twas there, on its side, Jesus

D. S.—suffered and died, To redeem a sinner like me.

5 Then the darkness came down,
   And the rocks rent around,
And a cry pierced the sad-laden air!
   'Twas the voice of our King,
   Who received death's dark sting,
All to save us from endless despair!

6 Let the sun hide its face,
   Let the earth reel apace,
Over men who their Saviour have slain!
   But, behold! from the sod,
   Comes the blest Lamb of God,
Who was slain, but is risen again!

Copyright, 1896, by Jno R. Sweney.

He Hideth my Soul.

FANNY J. CROSBY. WM. J. KIRKPATRICK.

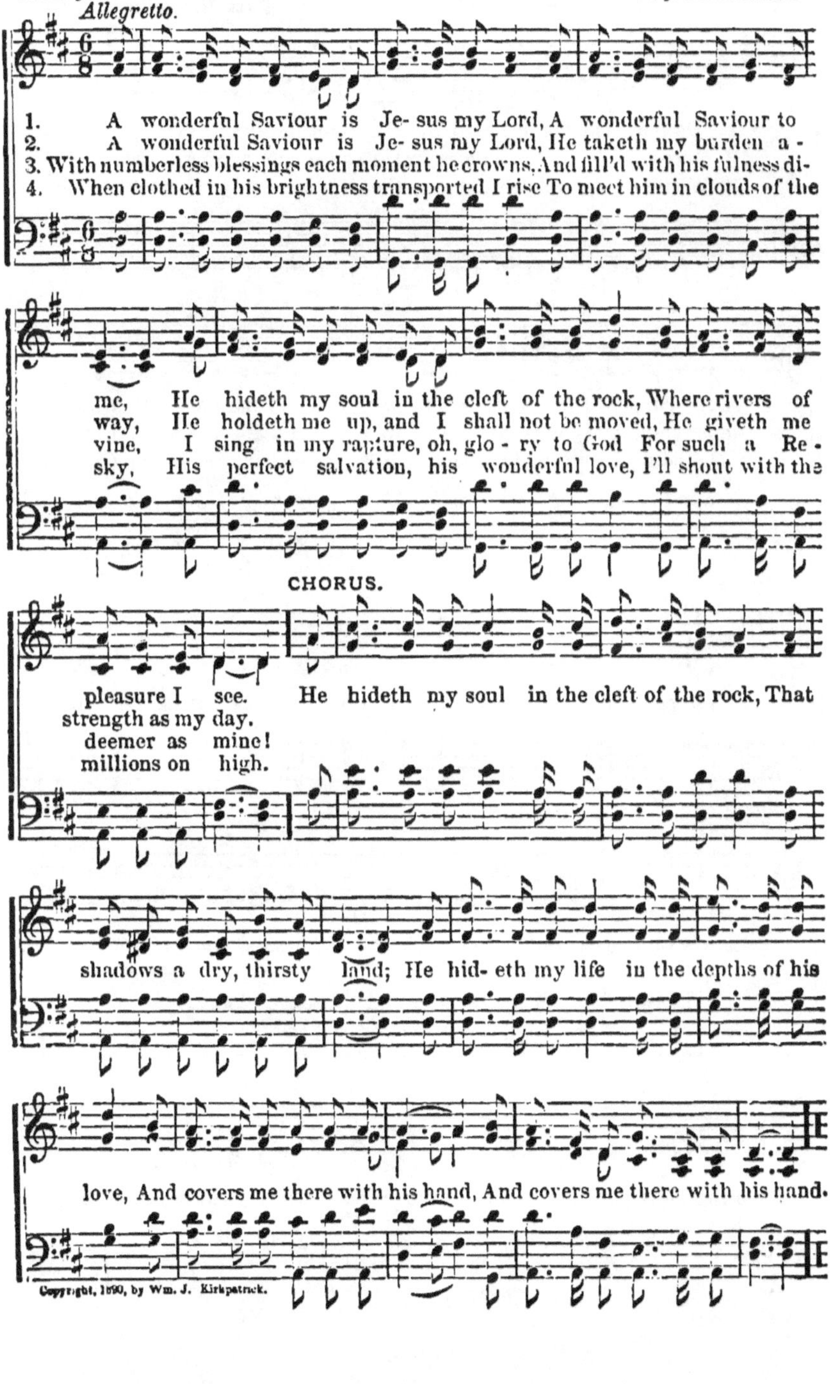

Allegretto.

1. A wonderful Saviour is Je-sus my Lord, A wonderful Saviour to me, He hideth my soul in the cleft of the rock, Where rivers of pleasure I see.
2. A wonderful Saviour is Je-sus my Lord, He taketh my burden a-way, He holdeth me up, and I shall not be moved, He giveth me strength as my day.
3. With numberless blessings each moment he crowns, And fill'd with his fulness di-vine, I sing in my rapture, oh, glo-ry to God For such a Re-deemer as mine!
4. When clothed in his brightness transported I rise To meet him in clouds of the sky, His perfect salvation, his wonderful love, I'll shout with the millions on high.

CHORUS.

He hideth my soul in the cleft of the rock, That shadows a dry, thirsty land; He hid-eth my life in the depths of his love, And covers me there with his hand, And covers me there with his hand.

Copyright, 1890, by Wm. J. Kirkpatrick.

I am Going up Yonder. 111

Rev. JOHNSON OATMAN, Jr.　　　　　　　　　　　　　　JNO. R. SWENEY.

1. I'm as happy as can be, for I'm go-ing home, Shortly over land and
2. With these eyes my blessed King I shall soon behold, With this voice I soon shall
3. Oh, how joyful it will be when I reach that land, Dear old comrades I shall
4. So, tho' pleasure with her smiles would entreat me stay, And tho' deep and heavy

sea I will no more roam; My house is now all ready where the joy bells ring,
sing on the streets of gold; My soul is pressing onward like a bird on wing,
see in that blood washed band; I soon will be among them and forever sing,
trials would impede my way, I'll count them all as nothing, but will onward spring;

D.S.—I soon will reach that country where the joy bells ring;

Fine. **CHORUS.**

I am go-ing up yonder to live with the King. Then vain world good-
[by, good-

by, I am going home, From that blessed land on high I will no more roam,

Copyright, 1896, by Jno. R. Sweney.

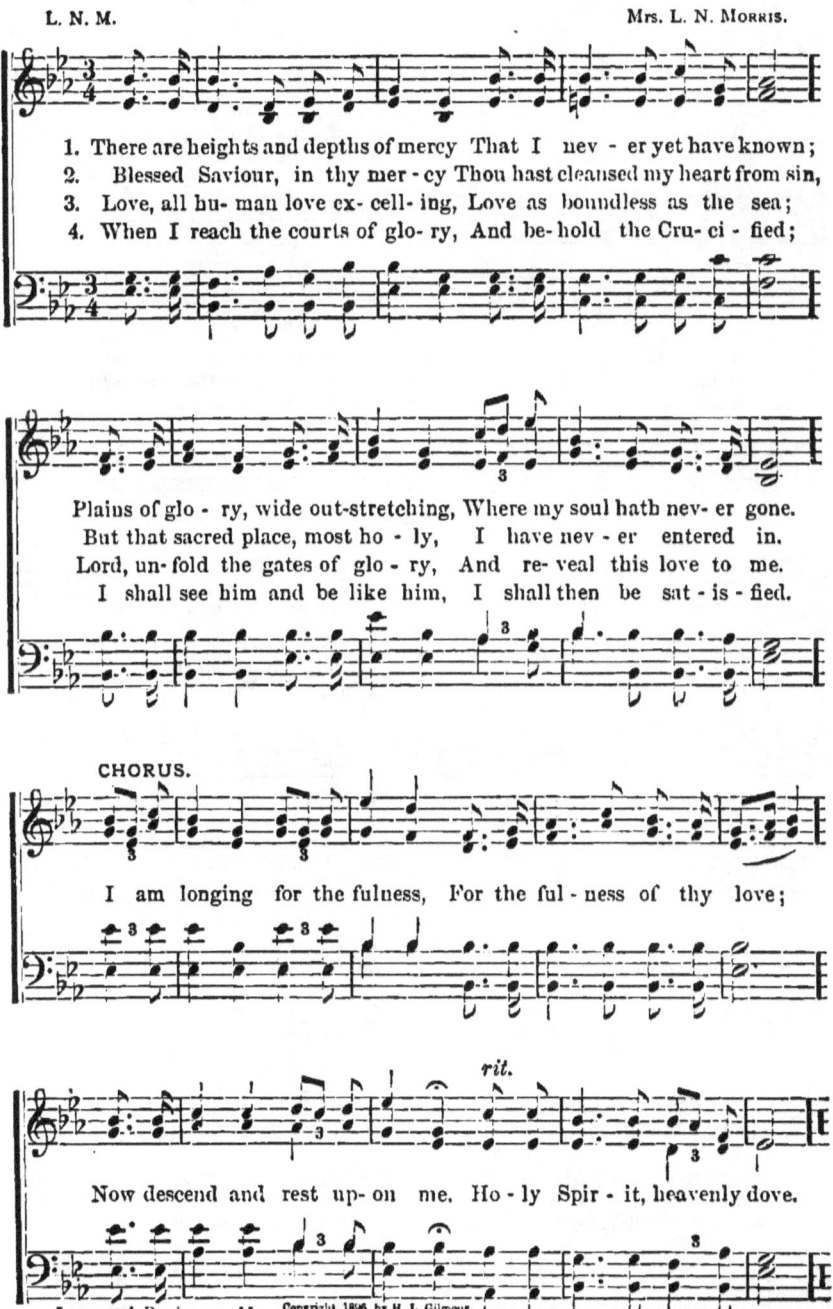

120. Forget Not.

E. E. Hewitt.   F. E. Belden.

1. Forget not the numberless mercies That sparkle in love's dia-dem, For even the night's sable mantle Is shining with many a gem.
2. Remember the way he hath led us, Thro' pastures all sunny and fair, Or, if thro' the desert of sorrow, The wellsprings of comfort were there.
3. Remember the burdens he lifted, The prayers that he turned into song, The blossoms that grew by the wayside, The heaven he'll give us ere long.

REFRAIN.

Forget not, O my soul! Forget not, O my soul! O let us give thanks to the Lord, O let us give thanks to the Lord, While threading his blessings like jewels, Threading his blessings like jewels, Threading his blessings like jewels On memry's golden cord.

Copyright, 1895, by John J. Hood.

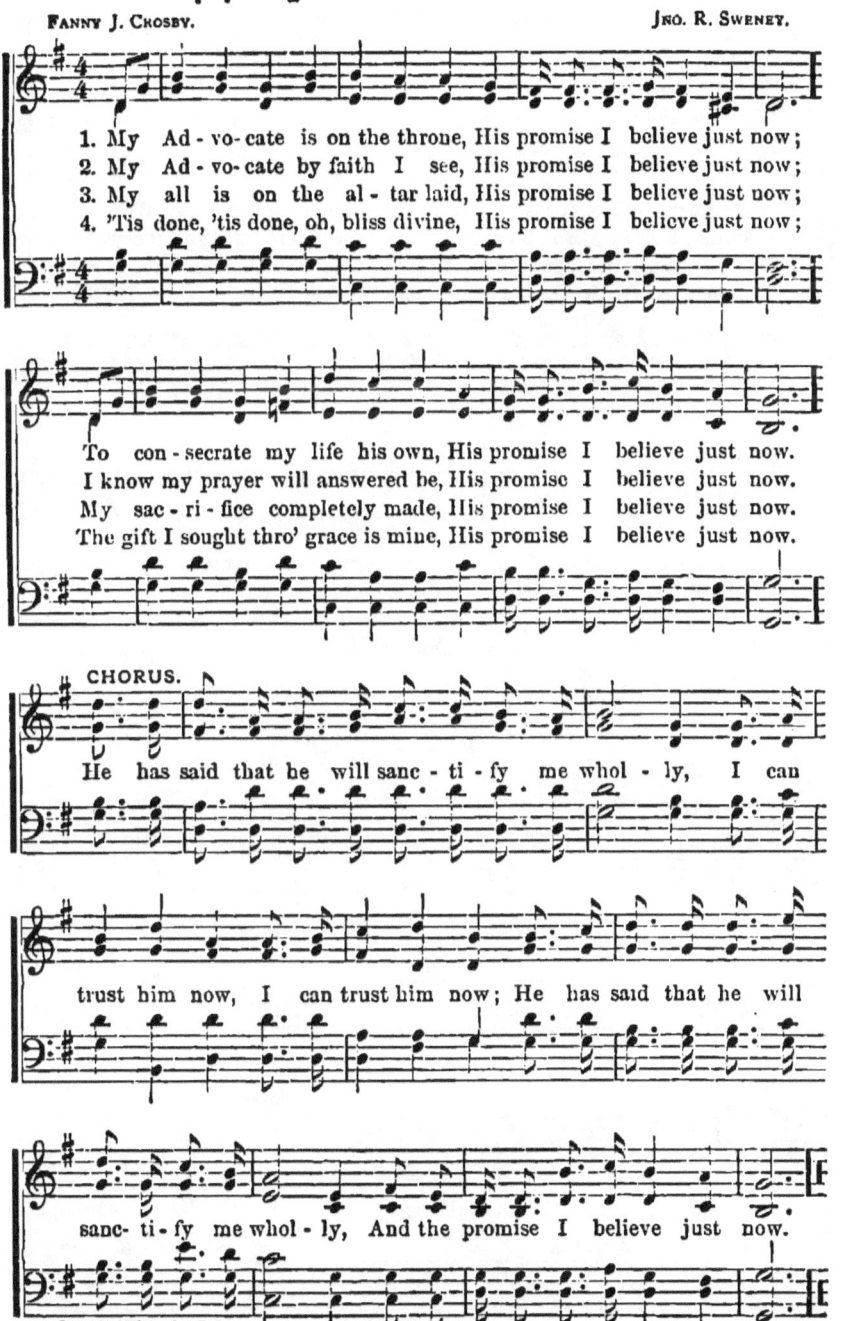

122. Over the Dead=Line.

When urging an exceedingly wicked man to flee from the wrath to come, I was met by this statement: "I was brought up to honor God, and I have ended by hating him; I have blasphemed his name, and resisted his Spirit until I can no longer repent or believe, if there is a dead-line to God's grace I have drifted over it, and am lost."—W. G. M.

VIRGINIA W. MOYER.　　　　　　　　　　　　　　　　　　　　　　H. L. GILMOUR.

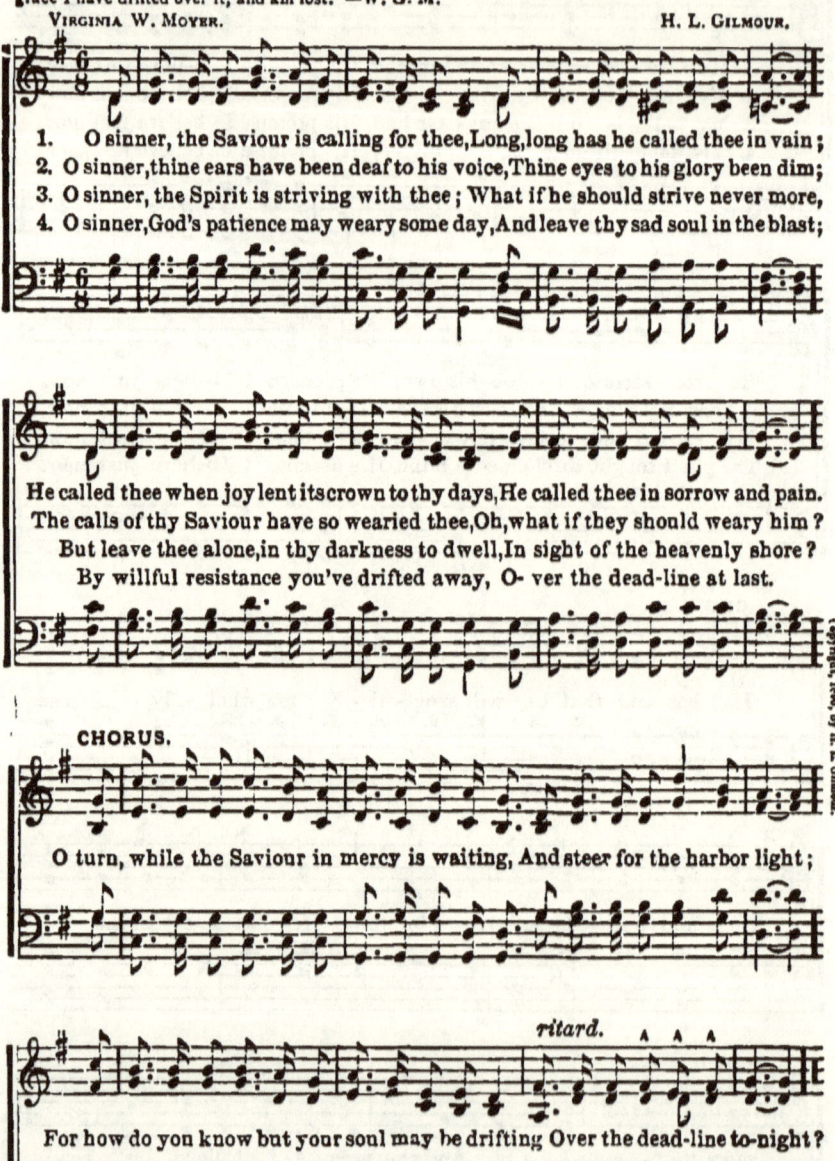

1. O sinner, the Saviour is calling for thee, Long, long has he called thee in vain;
2. O sinner, thine ears have been deaf to his voice, Thine eyes to his glory been dim;
3. O sinner, the Spirit is striving with thee; What if he should strive never more,
4. O sinner, God's patience may weary some day, And leave thy sad soul in the blast;

He called thee when joy lent its crown to thy days, He called thee in sorrow and pain.
The calls of thy Saviour have so wearied thee, Oh, what if they should weary him?
But leave thee alone, in thy darkness to dwell, In sight of the heavenly shore?
By willful resistance you've drifted away, O- ver the dead-line at last.

CHORUS.

O turn, while the Saviour in mercy is waiting, And steer for the harbor light;

ritard.

For how do you know but your soul may be drifting Over the dead-line to-night?

Copyright, 1906, by H. L. Gilmour.

Be Strong.

FANNY J. CROSBY.   **JNO. R. SWENEY.**

1. Be strong, O Christian soldiers, Lay not our armor down; Hold fast our faith un-
2. Rejoice, O Christian soldiers, Our watchword pass along; Till rank by rank, with
3. March on, O Christian soldiers, Our great Commander, near, Now waves aloft a
4. Look up, O Christian soldiers, Our time is waning fast; The cares our hearts op-

CHORUS.

daunted, Let no one take our crown. A few more foes to conquer, A few more
vigor, Takes up and swells the song.
signal That tells us not to fear.
pressing Will not forev-er last.

A few more foes to conquer,

storms to meet; And then, with him who loves us, Our resting will be sweet.
A few more storms to meet;

Copyright, 1890, by Jno. R. Sweney.

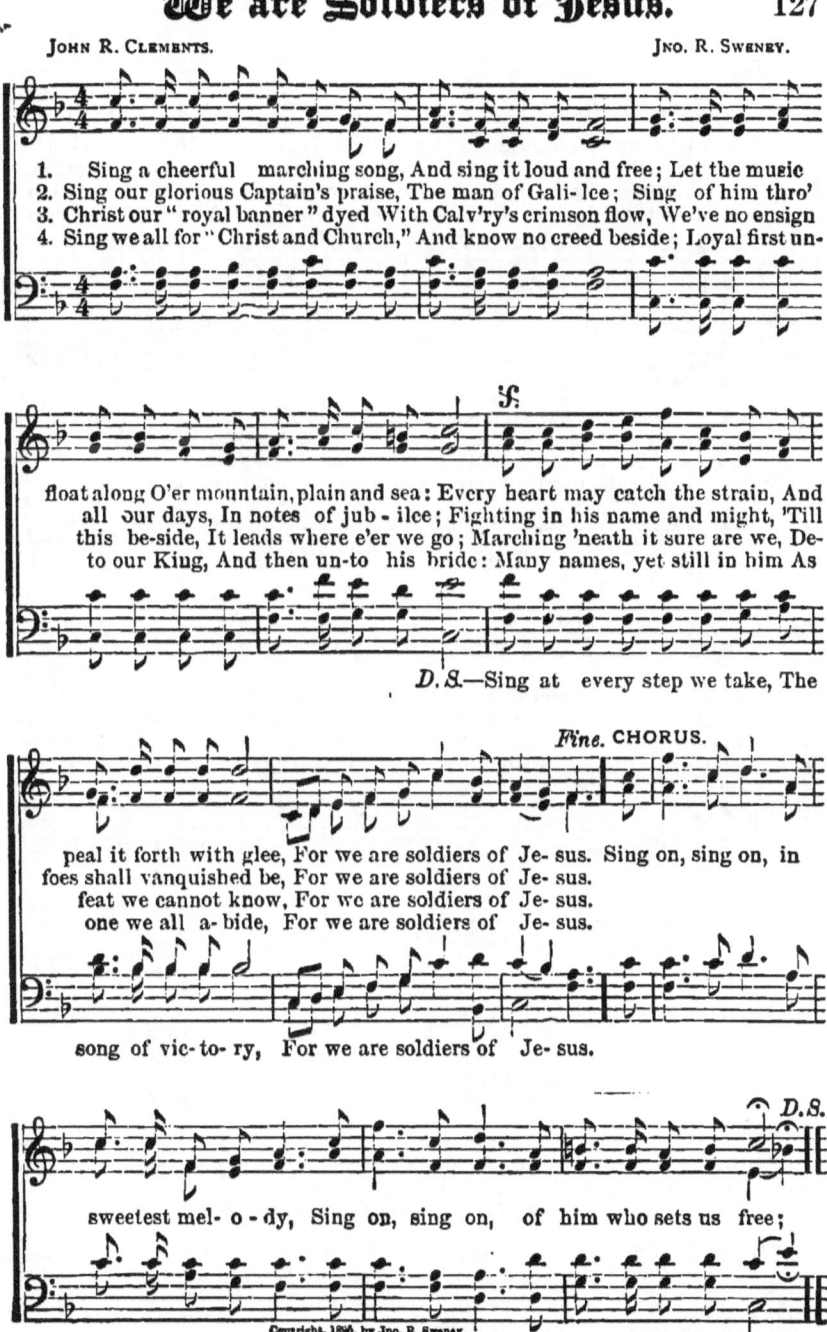

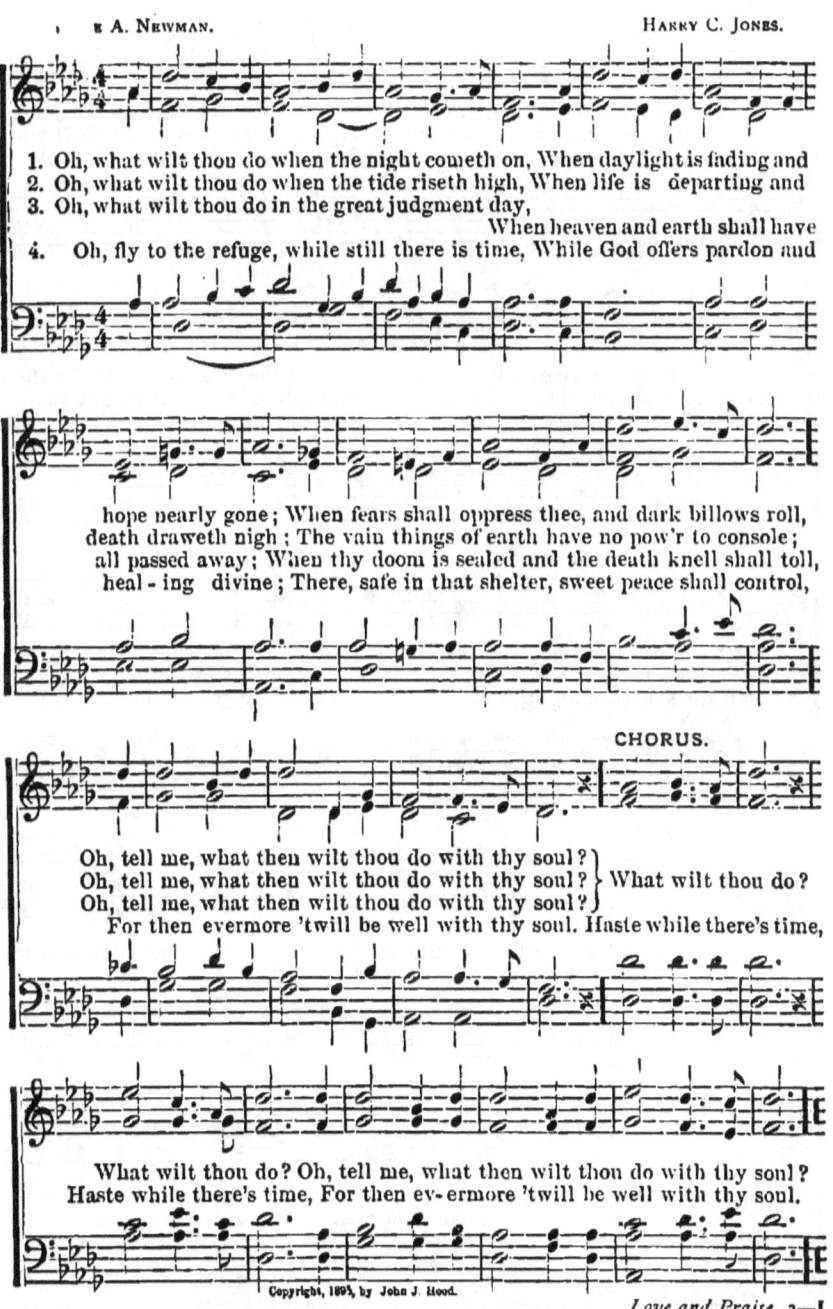

Gather the Sheaves.—CONCLUDED. 131

calling still, Onward with right good will, Gather the sheaves, gather the sheaves.
Gather the sheaves, gather the sheaves.

Jesus Guides Me All the Way.

W. J. S.
Rev. W. J Stuart, A. M.

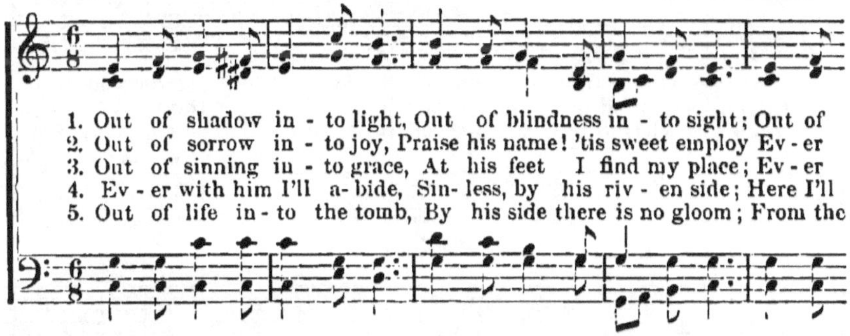

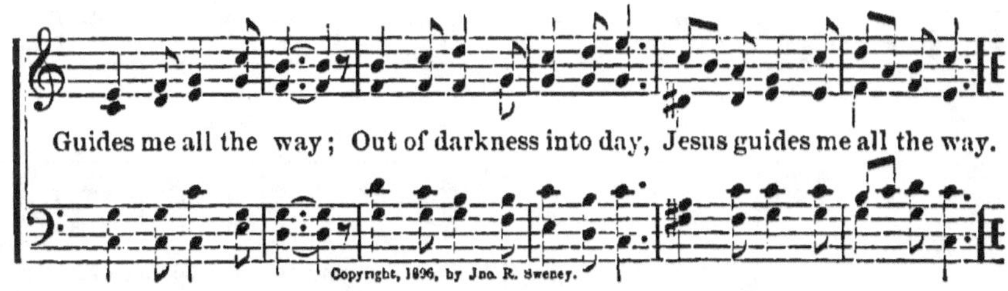

1. Out of shadow in-to light, Out of blindness in-to sight; Out of
2. Out of sorrow in-to joy, Praise his name! 'tis sweet employ Ev-er
3. Out of sinning in-to grace, At his feet I find my place; Ev-er
4. Ev-er with him I'll a-bide, Sin-less, by his riv-en side; Here I'll
5. Out of life in-to the tomb, By his side there is no gloom; From the

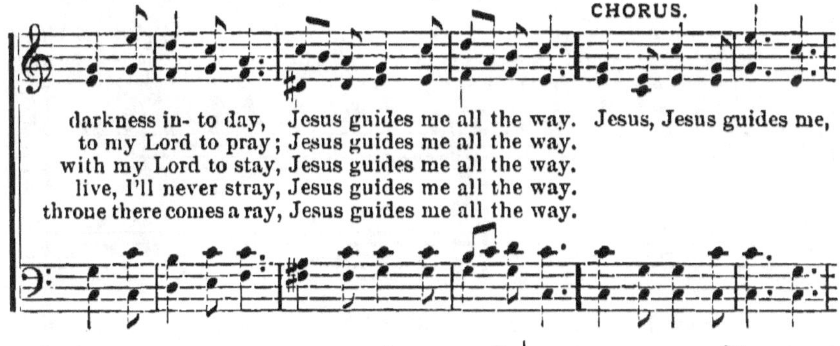

CHORUS.

darkness in-to day, Jesus guides me all the way. Jesus, Jesus guides me,
to my Lord to pray; Jesus guides me all the way.
with my Lord to stay, Jesus guides me all the way.
live, I'll never stray, Jesus guides me all the way.
throne there comes a ray, Jesus guides me all the way.

Guides me all the way; Out of darkness into day, Jesus guides me all the way.

Copyright, 1896, by Jno. R. Sweney.

6 Out of death to endless life,
Up from all the sin and strife;
Clothed upon with white array,
Jesus guides me all the way.

7 Up before the throne of gold,
I shall know a joy untold;
With the blood-washed I will **say,**
Jesus guided all **the way.**

I Love Him Far Better. 139

E. G. C.
Eli G. Christy.

1. It pays to serve Jesus, I speak from my heart; He'll always be with us, if we do our part; There's naught in this wide world can pleasure afford, There's peace and contentment in serving the Lord.
2. And oft when I'm tempted to turn from the track, I think of my Saviour,—my mind wanders back To the place where they nailed him on Calvary's tree— I hear a voice saying,— I suffered for thee!
3. There's a place that remembrance still brings back to me, 'Twas there I found pardon,—'twas heaven to me; There Jesus spoke sweetly to my weary soul, My sins are forgiven, he made my heart whole.
4. How rich is the blessing the world cannot give, I'm satisfied fully for Jesus to live, Tho' friends may forsake me and trials arise, I am trusting in Jesus—his love never dies.

D. S.—ever the cost, I'll be a true soldier,—I'll die at my post.

CHORUS.

{ I love him far better than in days of yore, } I'll do as he bids me what-
{ I'll serve him more truly than ever before, }

Copyright, 1894, by Jno R. Sweney.

5 Will you have this blessing that Jesus bestows,
A free, full salvation—as ev'ry one knows?
Oh, sinner, poor sinner, to Calvary flee,
The blood of my Saviour was shed there for thee.

6 There is no one like Jesus, can cheer me to-day, [away,
His love and his kindness can ne'er fade
In winter, in summer, in sunshine and rain, [same
His love and affection are always the

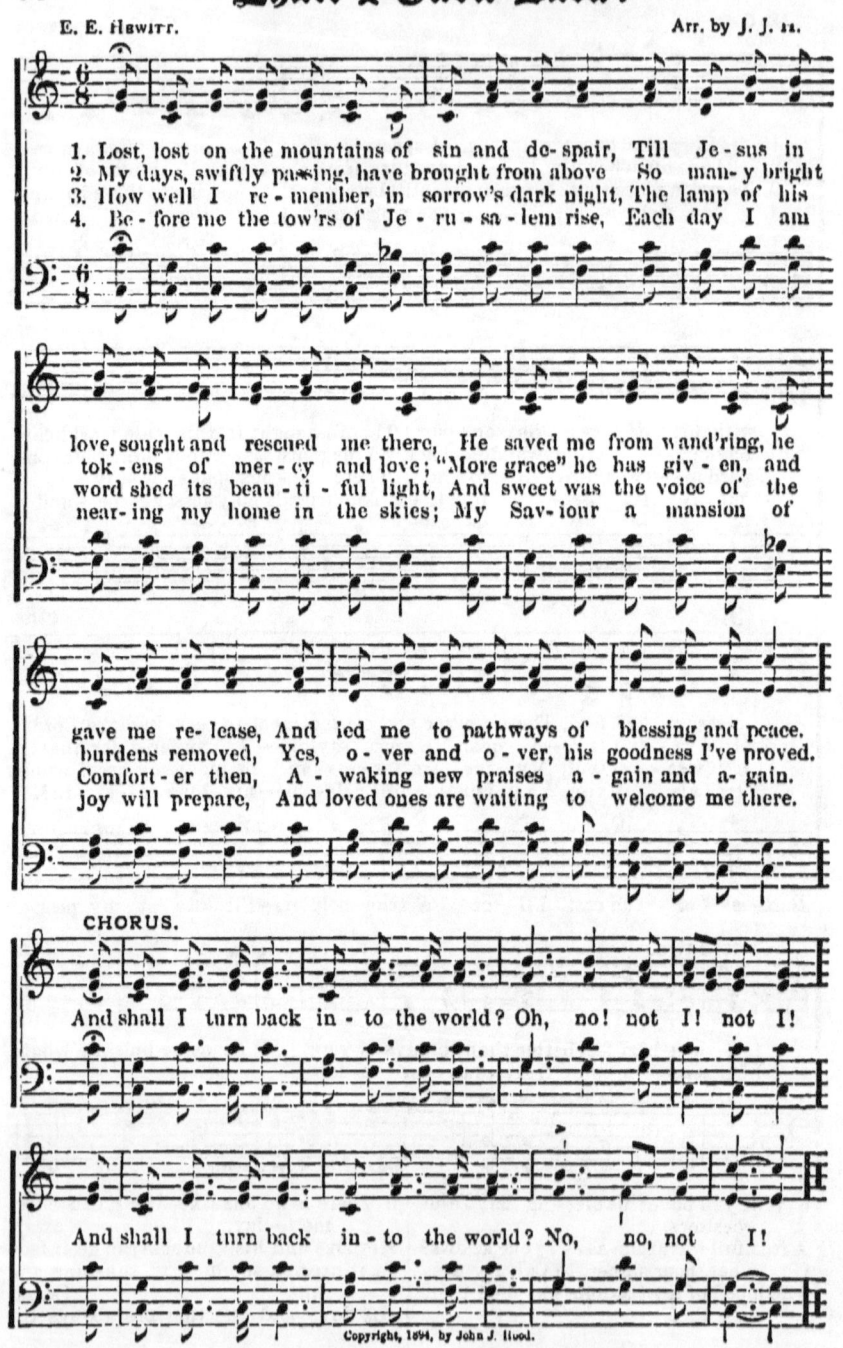

142. When the Curtains are Lifted.

Mrs. Annie Wittenmeyer.　　　　　　　　　　　　Wm. J. Kirkpatrick.

1. When the curtains are lifted, Oh, what shall I see? Will my Lord with his angels
2. Will the heaven-ly city Burst full on my sight; And the throne of his glory,
3. Now the future is hidden, I see but a pace, Yet it may be I'm nearing
4. When his glorified presence Shall gladden mine eyes, I'll be chang'd and be like him,

Be waiting for me? Will he welcome my coming, And crown me his own, With the
That giveth it light? Will the feet torn and weary Reach pavements of gold, And the
The end of the race; It will matter but little What changes may come, If my
And with him arise; And the hands hard with labor A victor's palm raise; And the

CHORUS.

(1, 2, 3.)
saints of all a-ges, That cir-cle his throne. When the curtains are lifted, Oh,
eyes red with weeping, The Saviour behold?
Lord with his angels Shall welcome me home.
lips tuned to sorrow Sing anthems of praise. (4.) When the curtains are lifted, Oh,

what shall I see? Will my Lord and his angels be waiting for me, Be wait -
this shall I see, That my Lord and his angels are waiting for me, Are wait -
　　　　　　　　　　　　　　　　　　　　　　　Be waiting for
　　　　　　　　　　　　　　　　　　　　　　　Are waiting for

ad lib.

· · · ing, be wait · · ing Will my Lord and his angels be waiting for me?
· · · ing, are wait · · ing, That my Lord and his angels are waiting for me?
me? be waiting for me?
me? are waiting for me?

Copyright, 1891, by Wm. J. Kirkpatrick.

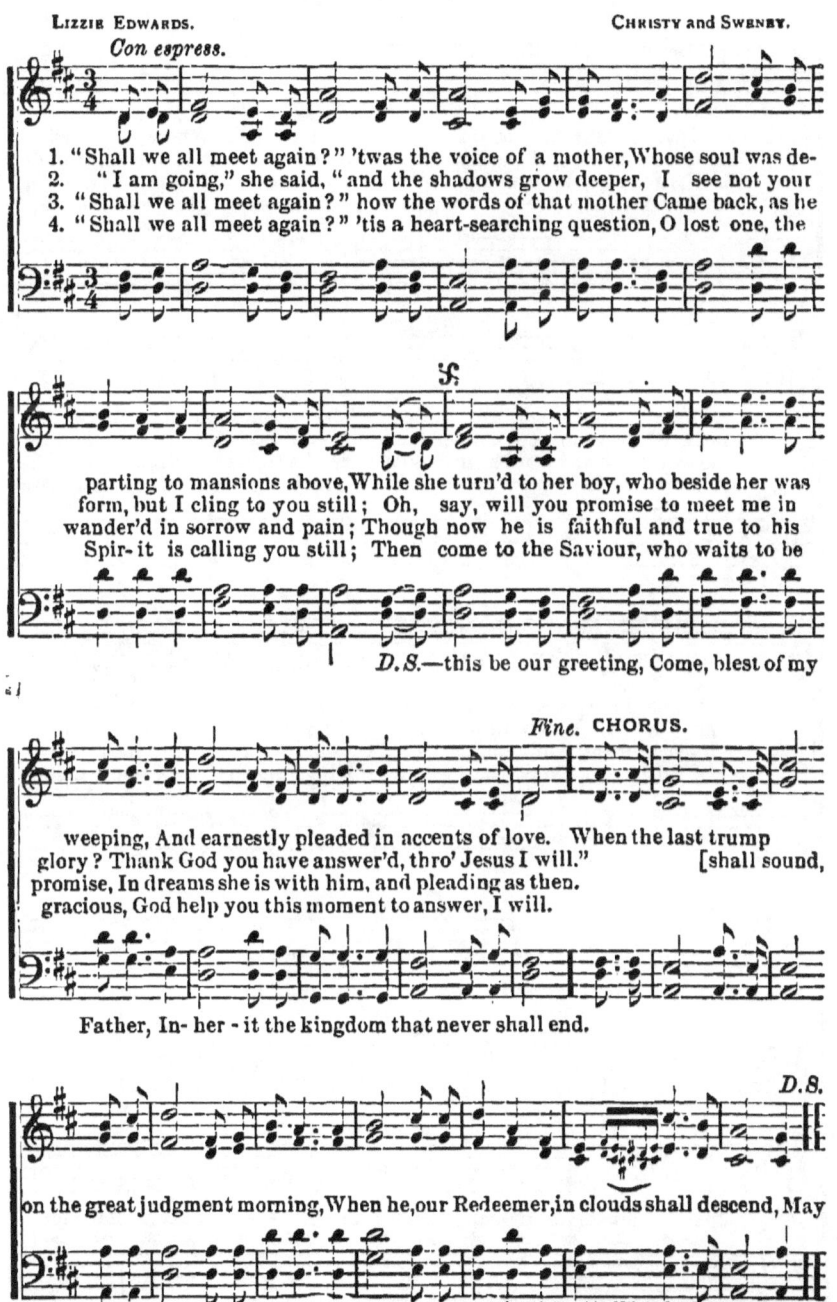

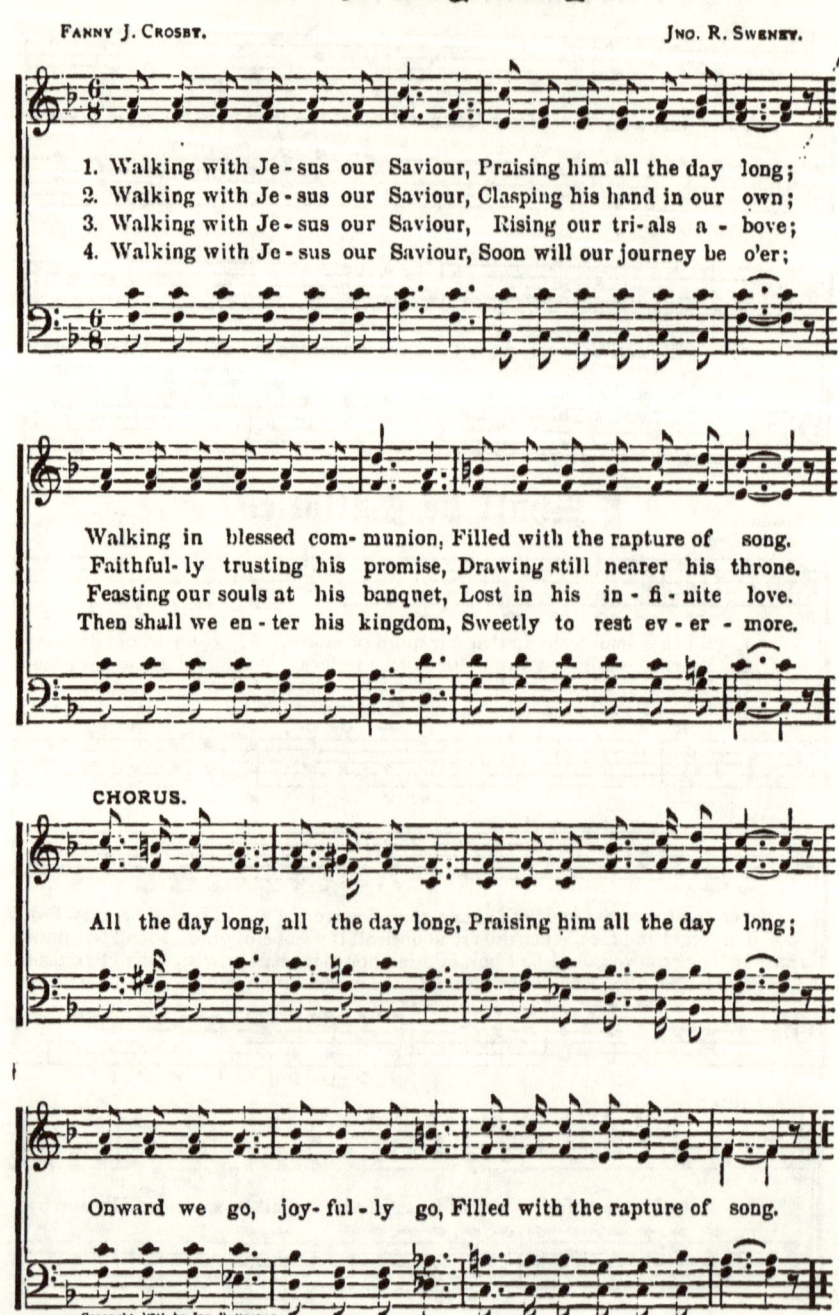

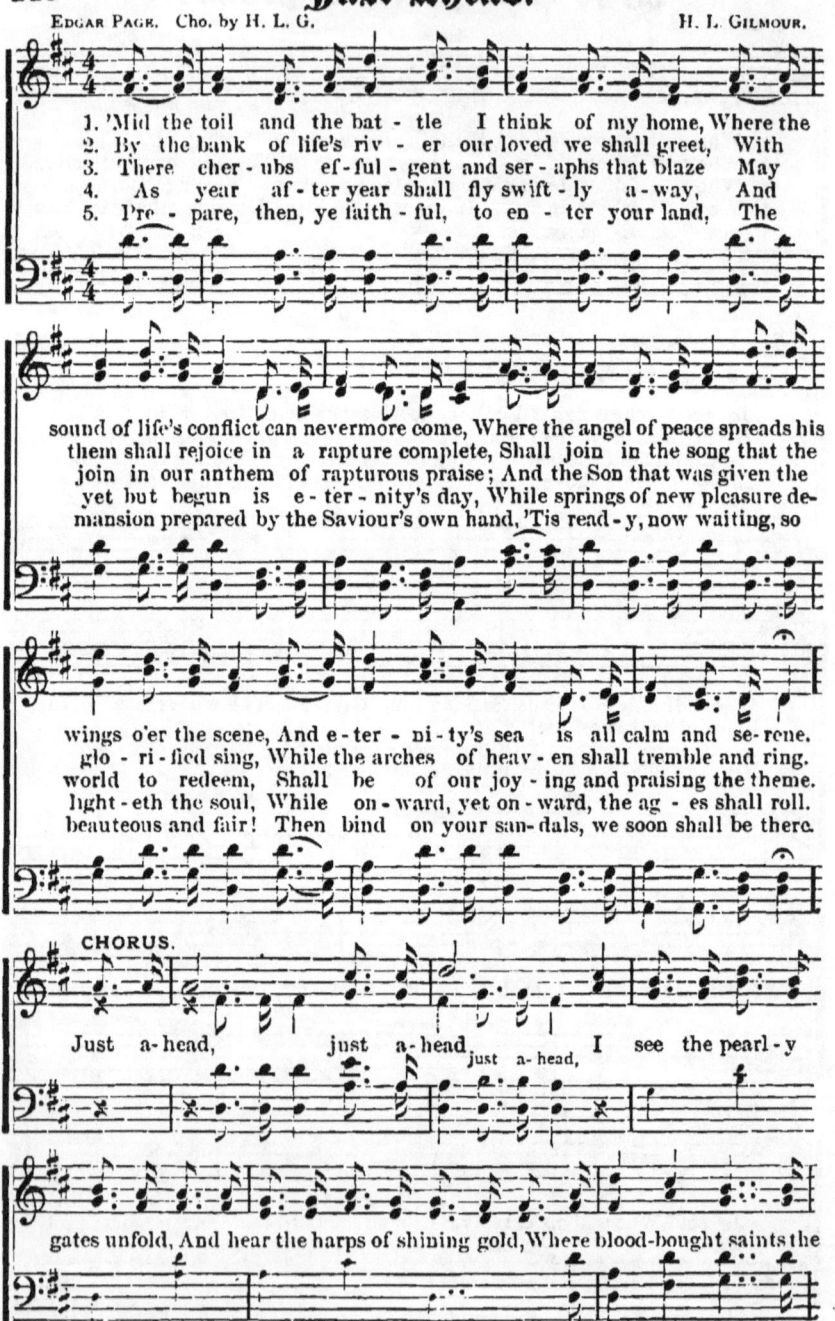

Just Ahead.—CONCLUDED. 149

new song sing To him who redeemed us, our bless-ed King.

Hallelujah, I'm Saved.

HENRIETTA E. BLAIR.   Adapted and arr. by WM. J. KIRKPATRICK.

1. How oft in holy converse With Christ, my Lord, alone, I seem to hear the
2. They pass'd thro' toils and trials, And tho' the strife was long, They share the victor's
3. My soul takes up the chorus, And pressing on my way, Communing still with
4. Thro' grace I soon shall conquer, And reach my home on high; And thro' eter-nal

CHORUS.

millions That sing around his throne:— Hal-le-lu-jah, I'm sav'd. Halle-
conquest, And sing the victor's song.
Je-sus, I sing from day to day:
a-ges I'll shout beyond the sky:

poco rit.

lu-jah, I'm sav'd. Hal-le-lu-jah, I'm sav'd. I'm sav'd, I'm sav'd.

Copyright, 1885, by Wm. J. Kirkpatrick.

150. Ashamed of Jesus.

Joseph Griggs.
E. O. Excell.

DUET.*

1. Je-sus, and shall it ev-er be, A mor-tal man ashamed of thee?
2. Ashamed of Je-sus! sooner far Let evening blush to own a star;
3. Ashamed of Je-sus! just as soon Let midnight be ashamed of noon;
4. Ashamed of Jesus! that dear friend, On whom my hopes of heav'n depend;
5. Ashamed of Je-sus! yes, I may, When I've no guilt to wash a-way,

Ashamed of thee, whom angels praise, Whose glories shine thro' endless days?
He sheds the beams of light divine O'er this benight-ed soul of mine.
'Tis midnight with my soul till he, Bright Morning Star, bids darkness flee.
No! when I blush be this my shame, That I no more revere his name.
No tear to wipe, no good to crave, No fears to quell, no soul to save.

CHORUS.

Ashamed .... of Je-sus, I never, I never will be; ....
Ashamed of Jesus, ashamed of Jesus, I never will be;

For Je - - - sus, my Sav - - iour, is not ashamed of me.
For Je-sus, my Saviour, for Je-sus, my Saviour,

Copyright, 1887, by E. O. Excell. By per.

*Ten. and Bass sing upper large notes; the Sop. and Alto the lower. Small notes with the large ones for organist.

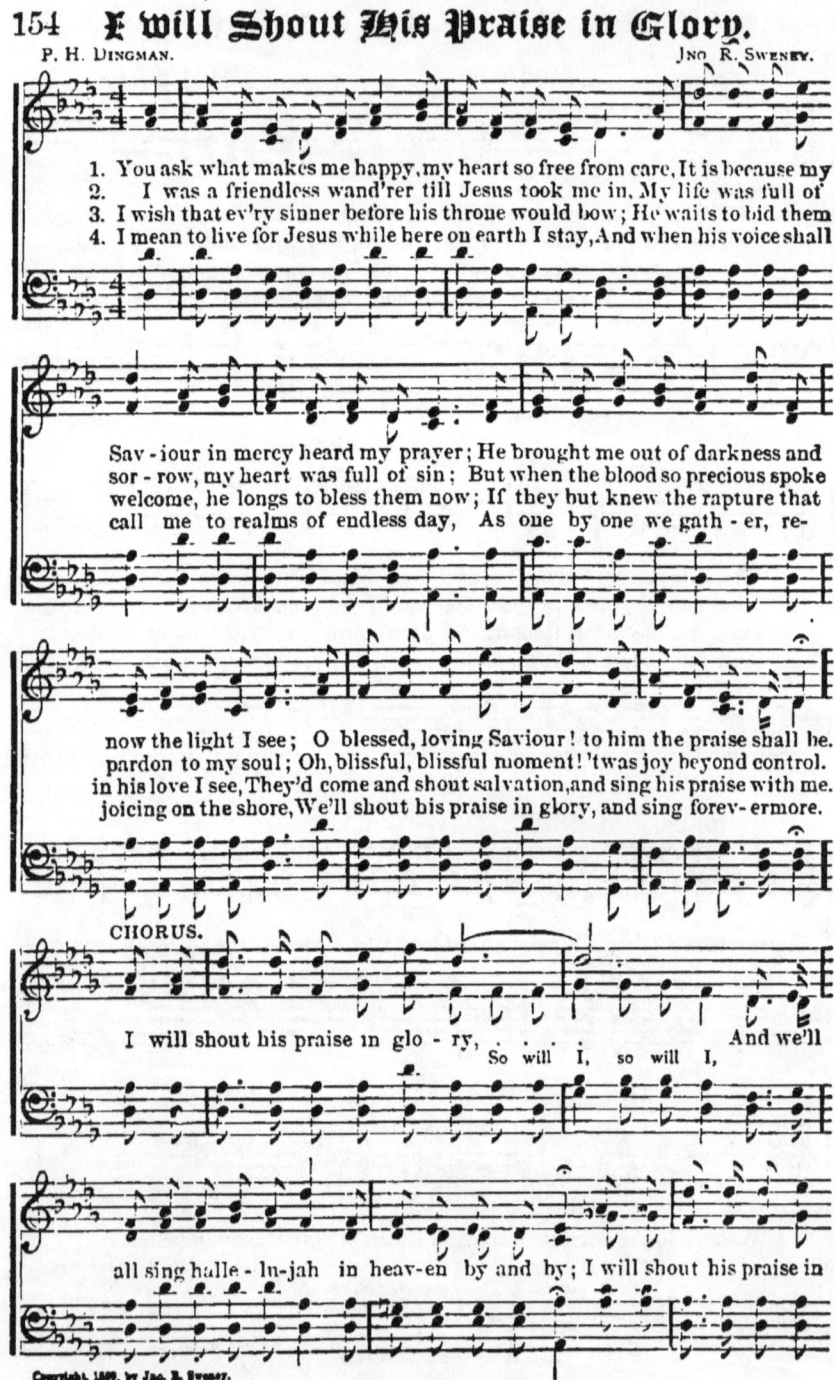

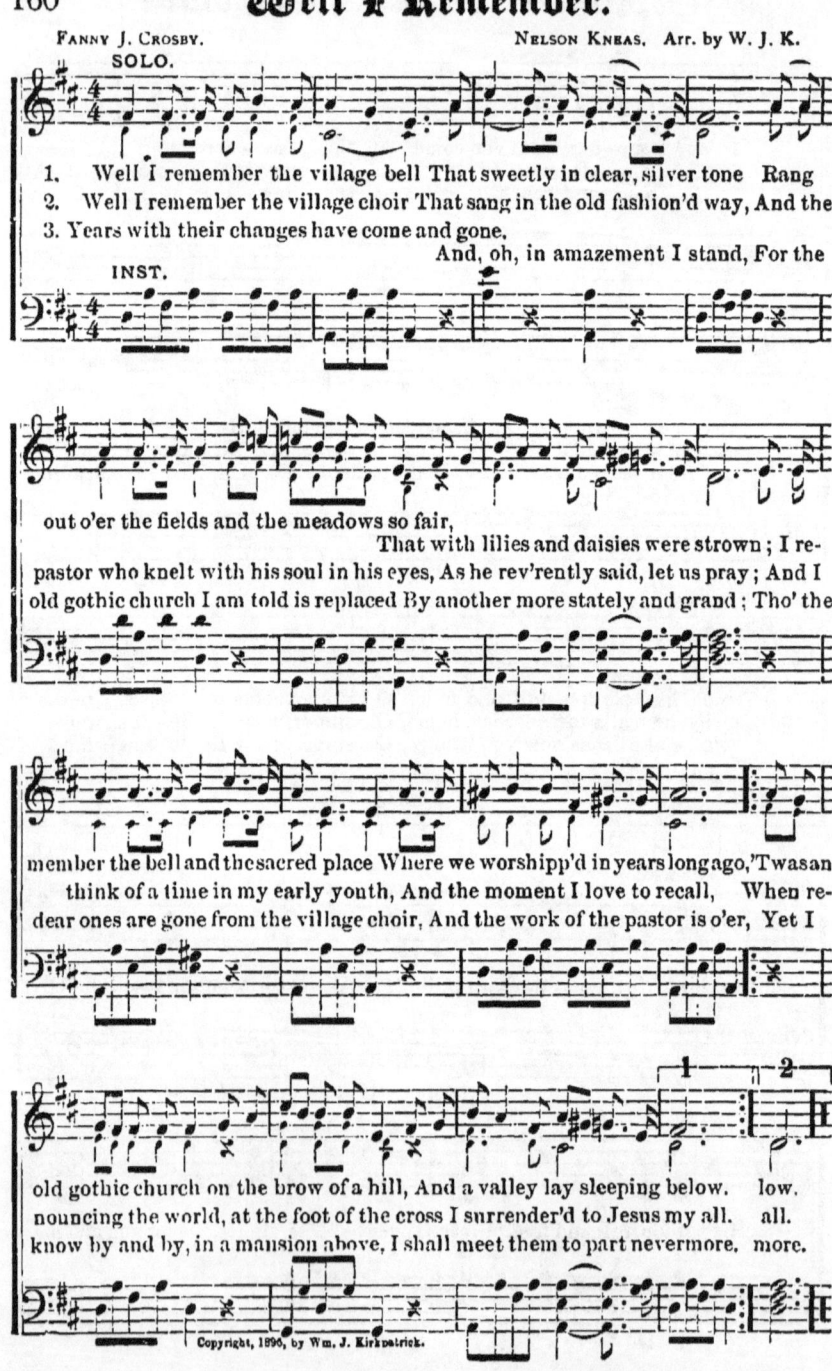

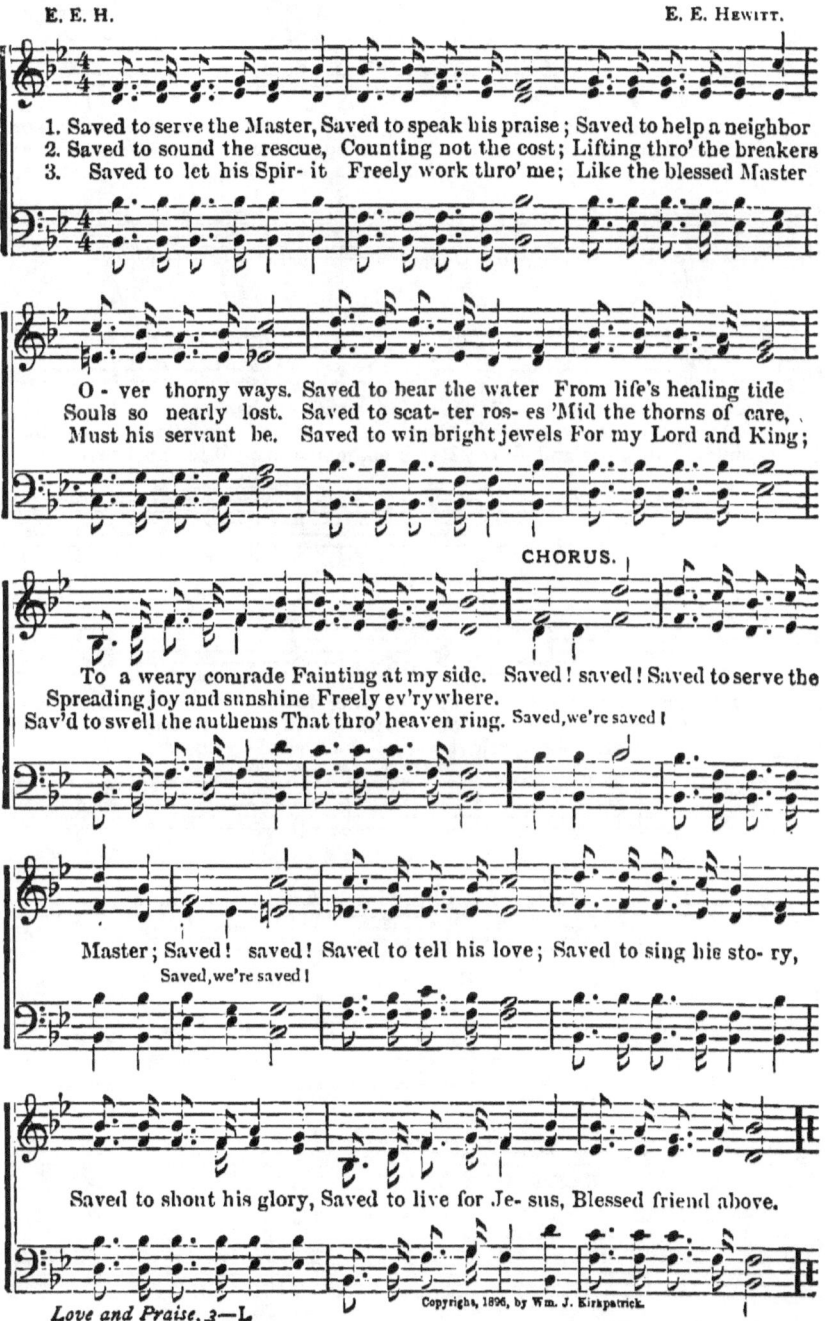

162. A Shout of Victory.

L. H. Edmunds.   Wm. J. Kirkpatrick.

1. March on, march on, follow the mighty Commander; March on, march on; Jesus our Captain and Lord; March on, march on; see that your steps never fal-ter, March on, march on, heeding his ev-'ry word.
2. March on, march on; joyful-ly singing, hosanna; March on, march on; fighting the bat-tle of faith; March on, march on; manfully bearing his ban-ner, March on, march on, faithful e'en un-to death.
3. March on, march on; still by his might overcoming; March on, march on; singing his glory and grace; March on, march on; till in the heaven-ly pal-ace, March on, march on, we shall behold his face.

CHORUS.

There's a song, that blends with prayer, There's a shout up-on the air; 'Tis a song of grace so

Copyright, 1890, by Wm. J. Kirkpatrick.

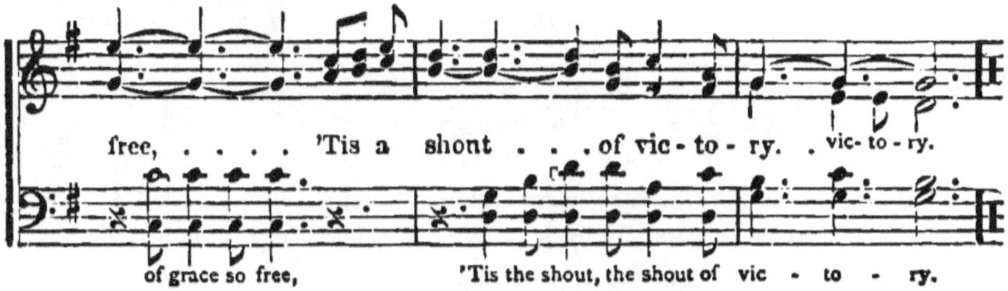

A Shout of Victory,—CONCLUDED.

free, ... 'Tis a shout . . . of vic-to-ry. . vic-to-ry.
of grace so free, 'Tis the shout, the shout of vic-to-ry.

Wonderful Peace.

L. H. E. "My peace I give unto you."—John xiv: 27. L. H. EDMUNDS.

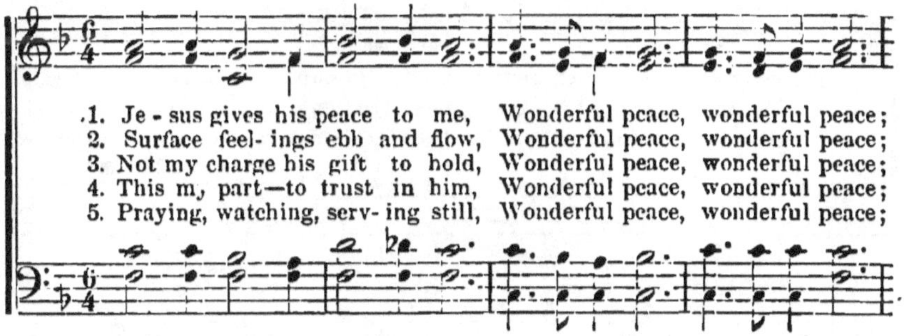

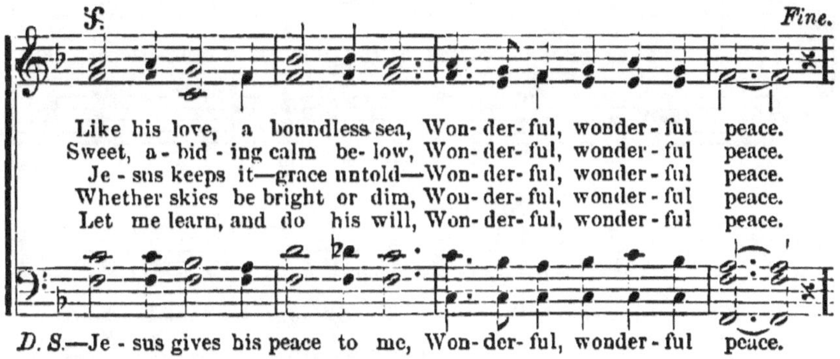

1. Je-sus gives his peace to me, Wonderful peace, wonderful peace;
2. Surface feel-ings ebb and flow, Wonderful peace, wonderful peace;
3. Not my charge his gift to hold, Wonderful peace, wonderful peace;
4. This my part—to trust in him, Wonderful peace, wonderful peace;
5. Praying, watching, serv-ing still, Wonderful peace, wonderful peace;

Like his love, a boundless sea, Won-der-ful, wonder-ful peace.
Sweet, a-bid-ing calm be-low, Won-der-ful, wonder-ful peace.
Je-sus keeps it—grace untold—Won-der-ful, wonder-ful peace.
Whether skies be bright or dim, Won-der-ful, wonder-ful peace.
Let me learn, and do his will, Won-der-ful, wonder-ful peace.

D. S.—Je-sus gives his peace to me, Won-der-ful, wonder-ful peace.

REFRAIN.   D.S.

Peace, peace, won-der-ful peace, Peace, peace, won-der-ful peace;

Copyright, 1896, by John J. Hood.

164. My Cup Runneth Over.

Rev. H. J. Zelley.   Psalm xxiii: 5.   H. L. Gilmour.

1. He gives me life, and home, and friends, My cup it runneth o-ver;
And mercies new each hour he sends, My cup it runneth o-ver.

2. New goodness and new mercies rare, My cup it runneth o-ver;
So constant is his loving care, My cup it runneth o-ver.

3. His word reveals the way of life, My cup it runneth o-ver;
And by his side I'm kept from strife, My cup it runneth o-ver.

CHORUS.

O bless-ed be my Shepherd, Friend, New pastures I dis-cov-er;
His lov-ing care will nev-er end, My cup it runneth o-ver.

Copyright, 1896, by H. L. Gilmour.

4 He guides my feet along the way,
  My cup it runneth over;
And helps me onward day by day,
  My cup it runneth over.

5 In pastures green my steps he leads,
  My cup it runneth over;
With bread of life my spirit feeds,
  My cup it runneth over.

6 He gives me drink from living streams,
  My cup it runneth over;
His love exceeds my wildest dreams,
  My cup it runneth over.

7 He calls me now his own, his bride,
  My cup it runneth over;
And draws me closer to his side,
  My cup it runneth over.

'Tis Burning in My Soul.—CONCLUDED. 167

glo-ry to his name! The fire of heav'nly love is burning in my soul.
burning in my soul.

Day by Day.

E. E. Hewitt.   Adam Geibel.
SOLO. *Andante.*

1. What praises shall I render, Day by day, For mercies, new and tender, Day by
2. My heart is fill'd with singing, Day by day; The bells of gladness ringing, Day by
2. May I, for others caring, Day by day, My Father's bounty sharing, Day by

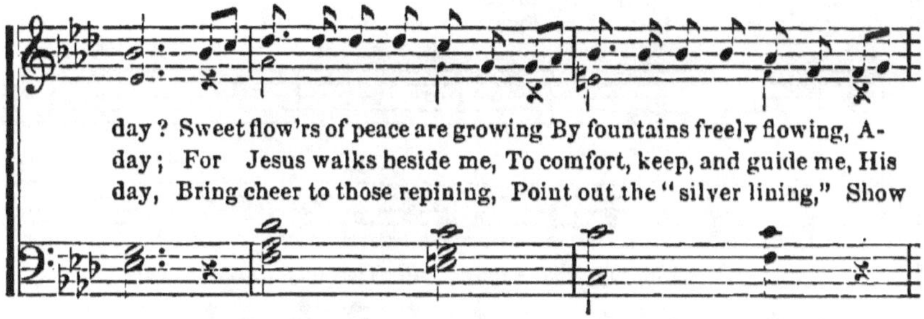

day? Sweet flow'rs of peace are growing By fountains freely flowing, A-
day; For Jesus walks beside me, To comfort, keep, and guide me, His
day, Bring cheer to those repining, Point out the "silver lining," Show

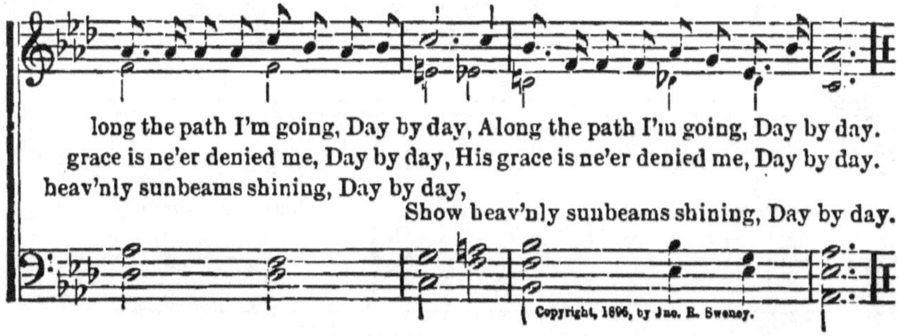

long the path I'm going, Day by day, Along the path I'm going, Day by day.
grace is ne'er denied me, Day by day, His grace is ne'er denied me, Day by day.
heav'nly sunbeams shining, Day by day,
                 Show heav'nly sunbeams shining, Day by day.

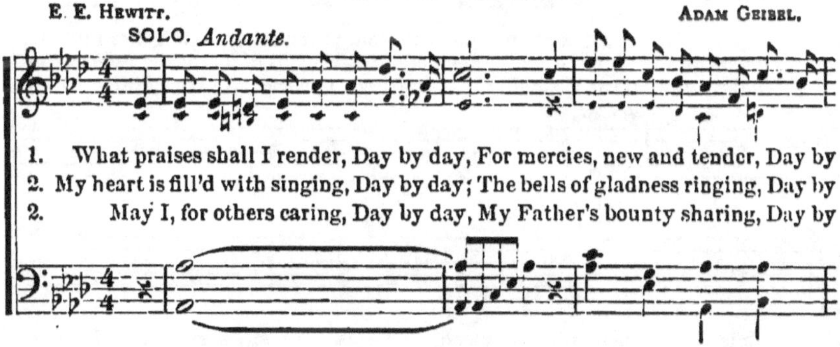

Copyright, 1896, by Jno. R. Sweney.

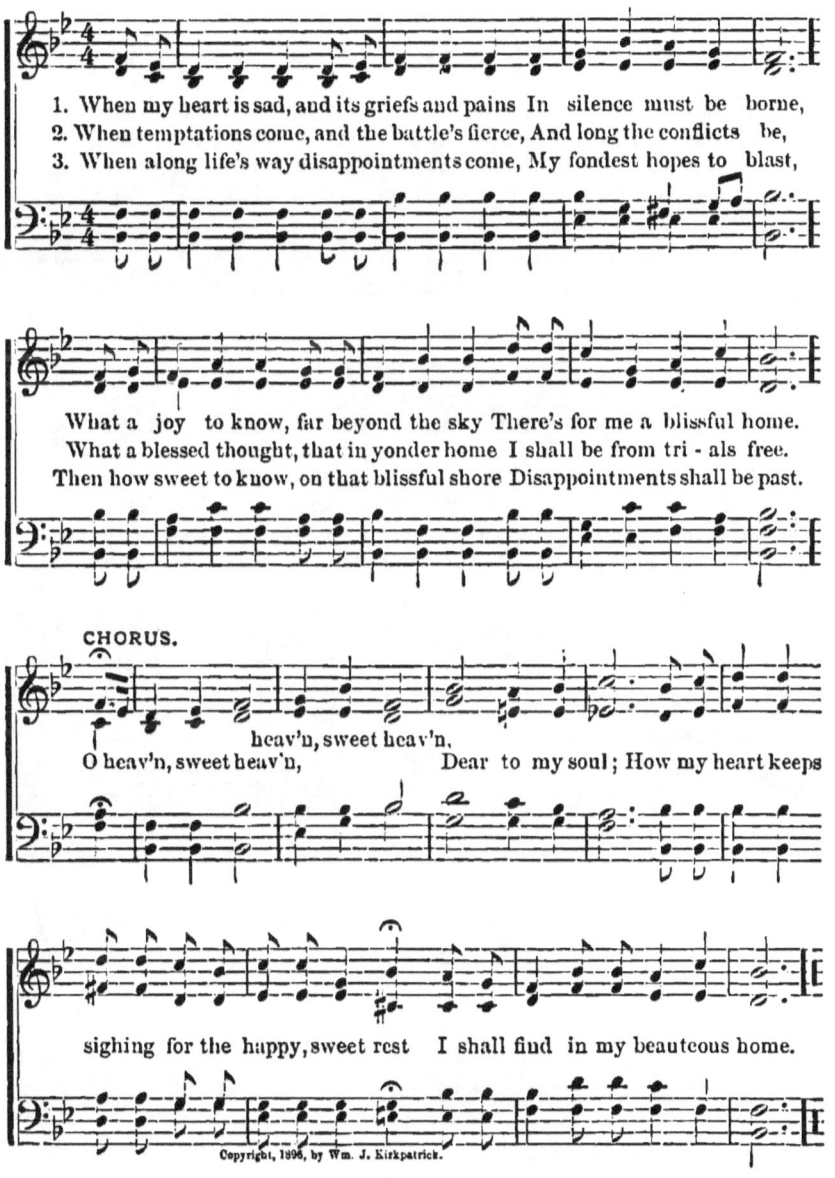

4 Tho' my friends forsake and I'm left a-
  Tho' age and want may come, [lone,
  I shall not forget that my Saviour's gone
  To prepare for me a home.

5 And when death shall come. and I lay
  Beneath the silent tomb, [me down
  I shall bid adieu to all pain and care,
  When I reach my happy home.

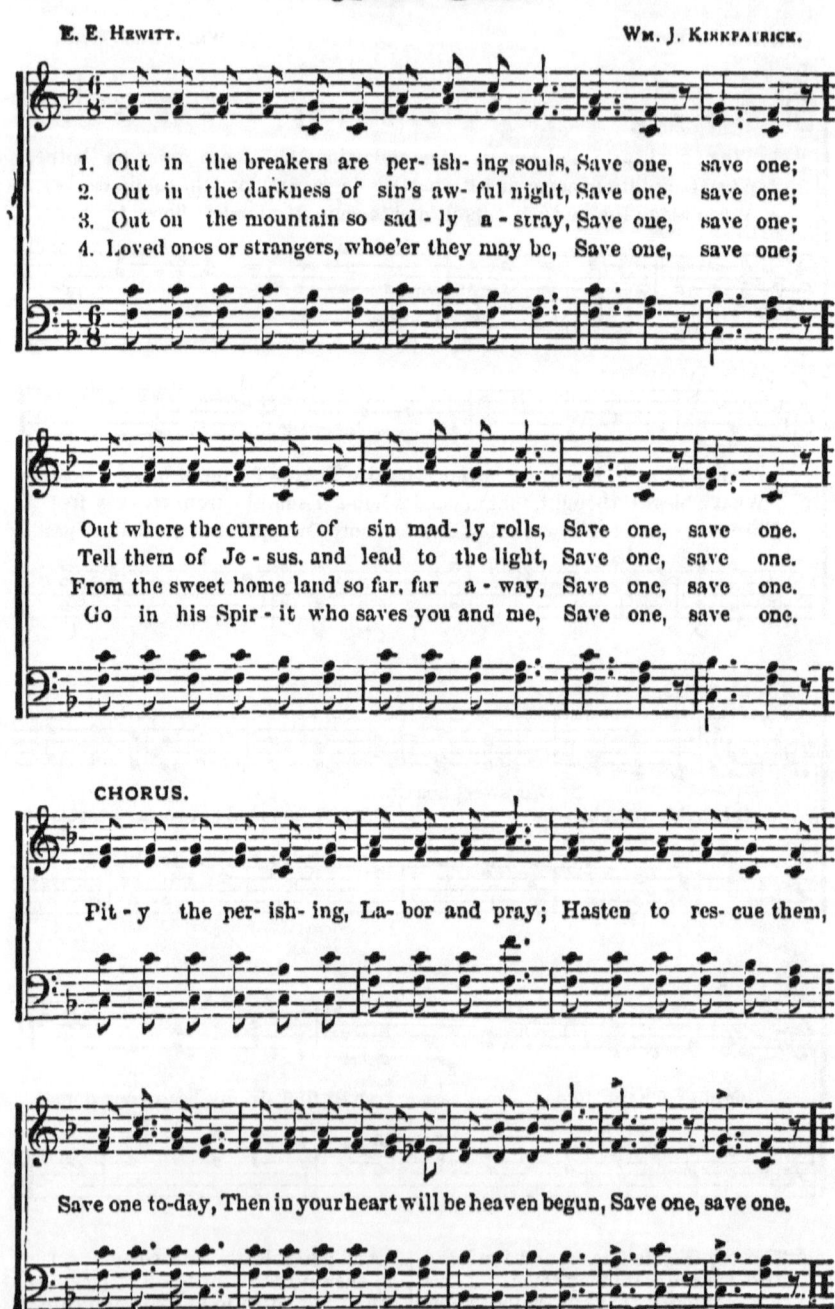

Leaning on the Everlasting Arms. 171

Rev. E. A. Hoffman.   A. J. Showalter.

1. What a fel-lowship, what a joy divine, Leaning on the ev-er-lasting arms; What a bless-ed-ness, What a peace is mine,
2. Oh, how sweet to walk in this pilgrim way, Leaning on the ev-er-lasting arms; Oh, how bright the path grows from day to day,
3. What have I to dread, what have I to fear, Leaning on the ev-er-lasting arms? I have bless-ed peace with my Lord so near,

REFRAIN.

Lean-ing on the ev-er-last-ing arms. Lean - ing,
Lean-ing on the ev-er-last-ing arms.
Lean-ing on the ev-er-last-ing arms.   Lean-ing on Je-sus,

lean - ing, Safe and se-cure from all a-larms;
Lean - ing on Je - sus,

Lean - ing, lean - ing, Leaning on the ev-er-lasting arms.
Lean-ing on Je-sus, lean-ing on Je-sus,

By par. A. J. Showalter.

That Old, Old Story is True.—CONCLUDED. 173

found out the reason they love it so well, That old, old sto-ry is true.
oh, what sweet peace in my heart since I found That old, old sto-ry is true.
peace to my soul, it is joy to my heart That old, old sto-ry is true.
mansion in glo-ry for all who beleive" That old, old sto-ry is true.

REFRAIN.

That old, old sto-ry is true, That old, old sto-ry is true; But I've
That old, old sto-ry is true, That old, old sto-ry is true; But
That old, old sto-ry is true, That old, old sto-ry is true; It is
That old, old sto-ry is true, That old, old sto-ry is true; "There's a
       it is true,   it is true,

found out the reason they love it so well, That old, old sto-ry is true.
oh, what sweet peace in my heart since I've found That old, old story is true.
peace to my soul, it is joy to my heart, That old, old sto-ry is true.
mansion in glo-ry for all who beleive" That old, old sto-ry is true.

I Love to Tell the Story.

1 I LOVE to tell the Story
 Of unseen things above,
 Of Jesus and his glory,
 Of Jesus and his love!
I love to tell the story!
 Because I know it's true;
It satisfies my longings
 As nothing else can do.
CHO.—I love to tell the story!
 'Twill be my theme in glory,
 To tell the Old, Old Story
 Of Jesus and his love.

2 I love to tell the Story!
 More wonderful it seems
Than all the golden fancies
 Of all our golden dreams;
I love to tell the Story!
 It did so much for me!
And that is just the reason
 I tell it now to thee.

3 I love to tell the Story!
 For those who know it best
Seem hungering and thirsting
 To hear it like the rest.
And when, in scenes of glory,
 I sing the New, New Song,
'Twill be—the Old, Old Story
 That I have loved so long.

I'll be with Thee.—CONCLUDED. 175

Halle- lu - jah, halle- lu - jah, Halle- lu - jah, praise the Lord!
Hallelujah, praise him! Hallelujah, praise him! Hallelujah,
Hal - le - lu - jah, hal - le - lu - jah,

There's Power in Jesus' Blood.

HOPE TAYAWAY.   WM. J. KIRKPATRICK.

1. My happy soul re-joic-es, The sky is bright above; I'll join the
2. I heard the blessed sto-ry Of him who died to save; The love of
3. His gracious words of pardon Were mu-sic to my heart; He took a-
4. I plunge beneath this fountain, That cleanseth white as snow; It pours from
5. Oh, crown him King forever! My Saviour and my friend; By Zi-on's

CHORUS.

heav'nly voices, And sing redeeming love. For there's pow'r in Jesus' blood,
Christ swept o'er me, My all to him I gave.
way my burden, And bade my fears depart.
Calv'ry's mountain, With blessing in it's flow.
crystal riv-er His praise shall never end.

Pow'r in Jesus's blood; There's pow'r in Jesus' blood To wash me white as snow.

Copyright, 1896, by Wm. J. Kirkpatrick.

The Best Friend is Jesus.—CONCLUDED. 177

Je - sus, He will help you when you fall, He will
Je- sus all the way;

hear you when you call; Oh, the best friend to have is Je - sus.

Consecration.

Mrs. MARY D. JAMES. Mrs. JOS. F. KNAPP.

1. My bo - dy, soul, and spirit, Jesus, I give to thee, A con-secrat-ed
2. O Jesus, mighty Saviour, I trust in thy great name, I look for thy sal-
3. Oh, let the fire, descending Just now upon my soul, Consume my humble
4. I'm thine, O blessed Jesus, Wash'd by thy precious blood, Now seal me by thy

REFRAIN.

offering, Thine ev-ermore to be. My all is on the al-tar, I'm
va-tion, Thy promise now I claim.
offering, And cleanse and make me whole.
Spir - it, A sac - rifice to God.

rit.
waiting for the fire; Waiting, waiting, waiting, I'm waiting for the fire.

From "Notes of Joy," by per.

Victory Through Grace.—CONCLUDED.

Yet to the true and the faithful Vict'ry is promised through grace.

Taste and See.

Psalm xxxiv: 8.

E. E. HEWITT. H. L. GILMOUR.

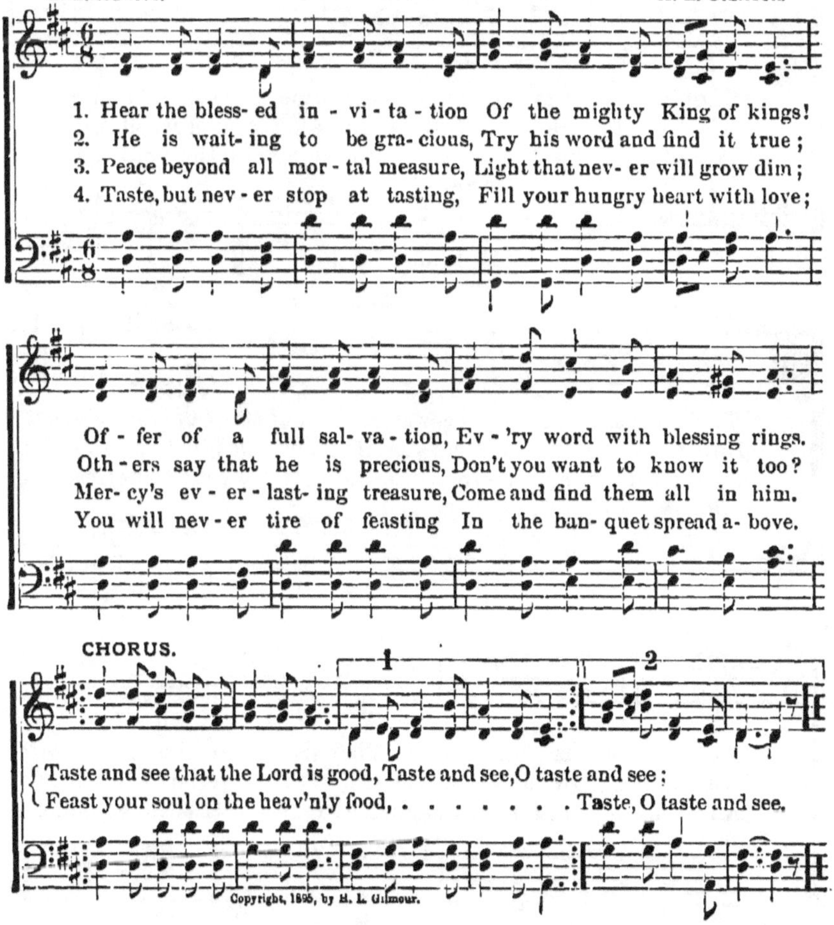

1. Hear the bless-ed in-vi-ta-tion Of the mighty King of kings!
2. He is wait-ing to be gra-cious, Try his word and find it true;
3. Peace beyond all mor-tal measure, Light that nev-er will grow dim;
4. Taste, but nev-er stop at tasting, Fill your hungry heart with love;

Of-fer of a full sal-va-tion, Ev-'ry word with blessing rings.
Oth-ers say that he is precious, Don't you want to know it too?
Mer-cy's ev-er-last-ing treasure, Come and find them all in him.
You will nev-er tire of feasting In the ban-quet spread a-bove.

CHORUS.

{ Taste and see that the Lord is good, Taste and see, O taste and see;
{ Feast your soul on the heav'nly food, ... Taste, O taste and see.

Copyright, 1895, by H. L. Gilmour.

184. Washed White as Snow.

Fanny J. Crosby.   *Jno. R. Sweney.*

1. Tho' my sins were once like crimson red, To the healing stream my feet were led,
2. At the door of faith I entered in, And to him confessed my guilt and sin,
3. Tho' my heart was all I had to give, Yet he smiled and bade me look and live;
4. I will sing his pow'r from death to save, I will sing his triumph o'er the grave,

In the precious blood my Saviour shed He washed me white as snow.
With his own dear hand he washed me clean, He washed me white as snow.
What a calm, sweet peace did I receive!—He washed me white as snow.
I will sing, while crossing Jordan's wave, He washed me white as snow.

CHORUS.

O, my joy-ful song henceforth shall be, 'Tis the blood of Je-sus cleanseth me, Cleanseth, cleans-eth, Oh, yes, it cleanseth me.

Copyright, 1880, by John J. Hood.

186. At Mother's Grave.

CARRIE ELLIS BRECK.   H. L. GILMOUR.

1. Far a-way from home and mother, Far a-way from peace and God;
2. When they told me she was dy-ing, Not till then would I re-lent;
3. Would that I once more could see her, Or could make her soul a-ware
4. Now my mother's in that cit-y, 'Mid the splendors of the throne,

Far from love and pray'r and blessing, In the path of sin I trod.
With my heart all bruis'd and bleeding, Bit-ter-ly did I la-ment.
That at last I came, re-penting, To the Lord that answers prayer.
O-verjoyed when an-gels tell her Je-sus sav'd her wayward son.

Oh, how oft I thought of mother, And her pray'rs that God would save,
Vain was all im-passioned weeping, Vain my pray'rs her life to save;
Oh, what love, what great compassion! He my ma-ny sins for-gave,
Oh, what bursts of hal-le-lujahs, When we meet the Lord who gave

ritard.

But my sin-ful heart was burden'd, Till I knelt at mother's grave.
In the churchyard she was sleeping, And I knelt at mother's grave.
For the sake of Christ my Saviour, When I knelt at mother's grave.
Peace and par-don to a wand'rer, When he knelt at mother's grave.

Copyright, 1906, by H. L. Gilmour.

Jesus Leads.

"And when he putteth forth his own sheep, he goeth before them, and the sheep follow him; for they know his voice."—John x: 4.

JOHN R. CLEMENTS.   JNO. R. SWENEY.

Andante.

1. Like a shepherd, tender, true, Jesus leads, ... Jesus leads, ...
2. All a-long life's rugged road Jesus leads, ... Jesus leads, ...
3. Thro' the sun-lit ways of life Jesus leads, ... Jesus leads, ...

Daily finds us pastures new, Jesus leads, ... Jesus leads; ...
Till we reach yon blest a-bode, Jesus leads, ... Jesus leads; ...
Thro' the war-ings and the strife Jesus leads, ... Jesus leads; ...

If thick mists are o'er the way, ... Or the flock 'mid danger feeds, ...
All the way, before, he's trod, And he now the flock precedes, ...
When we reach the Jordan's tide, Where life's bound-'ry-line re-cedes, ...

rit.

He will watch them lest they stray, Jesus leads, ... Jesus leads.
Safe in-to the fold of God Jesus leads, ... Jesus leads.
He will spread the waves a-side, Jesus leads, ... Jesus leads.

Copyright, 1893, by Jno. R. Sweney.

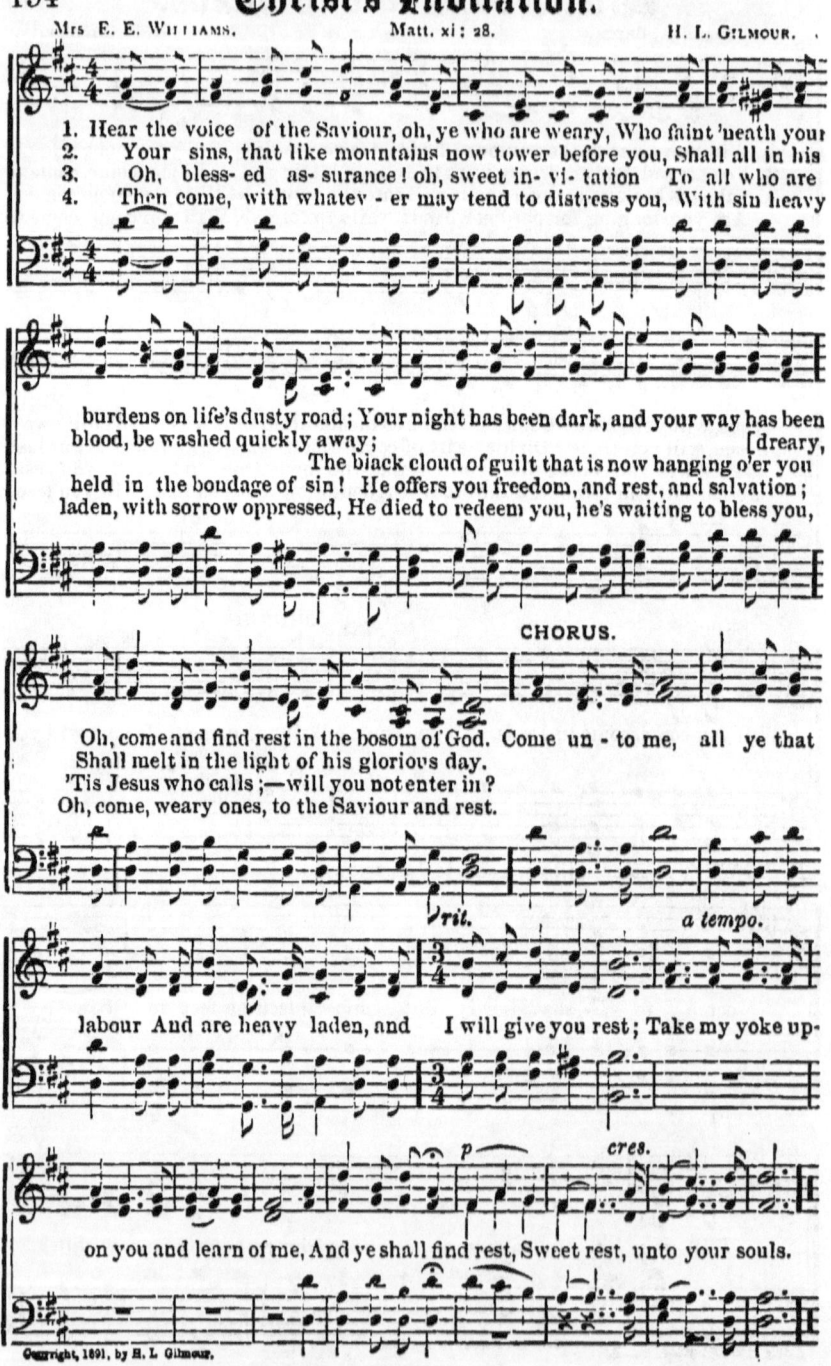

Onward, Christian Soldiers! 197

SABINE BARING-GOULD.   Tune, ONWARD. 6, 5.

1. Onward, Christian soldiers! Marching as to war, With the cross of Jesus
2. At the sign of triumph Satan's host doth flee; On, then, Christian soldiers,
3. Like a mighty army Moves the Church of God; Brothers, we are treading

Go-ing on be-fore. Christ, the royal Mas-ter, Leads against the foe;
On to vic-to-ry! Hell's foundations qiv-er At the shout of praise;
Where the saints have trod; We are not di-vid-ed, All one bo-dy we,

CHORUS.

Forward into bat-tle, See, his banners go!
Brothers, lift your voices, Loud your anthems raise.   Onward, Christian soldiers!
One in hope and doctrine, One in chari-ty.

Marching as to war, With the cross of Je-sus Going on be-fore.

4 Crowns and thrones may perish,
   Kingdoms rise and wane,
But the Church of Jesus
   Constant will remain;
Gates of hell can never
   'Gainst that Church prevail;
We have Christ's own promise,
   And that cannot fail.

5 Onward, then, ye people!
   Join our happy throng,
Blend with ours your voices
   In the triumph-song;
Glory, laud, and honor
   Unto Christ the King,
This through countless ages
   Men and angels sing.

198. In the Lord is our Hope.

MARTHA J. LANKTON.   WM. J. KIRKPATRICK.

1. In the Lord is our hope, On his word we are stayed, With its truth our de-
2. In the Lord is our trust, And his name we a-dore, For his kingdom shall
3. In the Lord is our strength, And we dread not our foes; We shall conquer thro'
4. In the Lord is our rest; Oh, the joy we shall see When his welcome we

CHORUS.

fense We shall not be dismayed. Hal-le-lu-jah! hal-le-lu-jah! Oh, ex-
stand When the world is no more.
grace, Though a host may oppose.
hear, And from toil we are free.

alt him a-gain! Hal-le-lu-jah in the highest, Halle-lu-jah, a-men.

Copyright, 1893, by Wm. J. Kirkpatrick.

199. Choose the Saviour.

"Choose you this day whom ye will serve."—Josh. xxiv: 17.

H. L. G.   H. L. GILMOUR.

1. Come to Je-sus, wand'rer, come, Still he waits to welcome home;
2. Come to Je-sus as you are, Break from Satan's ev-'ry snare,
3. Come to Je-sus, why decline Love's fond pleadings, heart of thine?
4. Come to Je-sus, now re-lent, Come, be-liev-ing-ly re-pent;
*5. Hal-le-lu-jah, Je-sus saves! Sing it loud, ye ransomed slaves;

Copyright, 1898, by H. L. Gilmour.

* If sung as a Solo the 5th verse to be sung by Choir and Congregation.

Choose the Saviour.—CONCLUDED.

From your life of sin and loss, Weep your way beneath the cross;
He enlists, but to enslave; Jesus woos, and woos to save:
Calv'ry, tinged with sacred blood, Now invites to heaven and God;
Come, submissive to his sway, Come, our Captain wins to-day;
Calv'ry's victim ever wins, Death and hell in malice grins,

Choose the Saviour, hear his voice, Come, repent, believe, rejoice.
Fly into his pierced embrace; Be a sinner saved by grace.
Hear the invitation sweet, Come, surrender at his feet.
Sin a captive has been led, Christ has bruised the serpent's head.
For a brand is snatched away From sin's night to endless day.

200 Whate'er it Be.

ELTA M. LEWIS. "Thy will be done." WM. J. KIRKPATRICK.

1. I take my portion from thy hand, And do not seek to understand;
2. When darkness doth thy face obscure, And many sorrows I endure,
3. When tender joys to me are known, I render thanks to thee alone;
4. Thus calmly do I face my lot, Accept it, Lord, and doubt thee not;

CHO.—Whate'er it be! whate'er it be! I do not fear, whate'er it be;

D. C. Chorus.

For I am blind, while thou dost see, Thy will is mine, whate'er it be.
I think of Christ's Gethsemane; Thy will is mine, whate'er it be.
I know my cup is filled by thee; Thy will is mine, whate'er it be.
Lo! all things work for good to me; Thy will is mine, whate'er it be.

Copyright, 1893, by Wm. J. Kirkpatrick.

Thy love divine sustaineth me, Thy will is mine, whate'er it be.

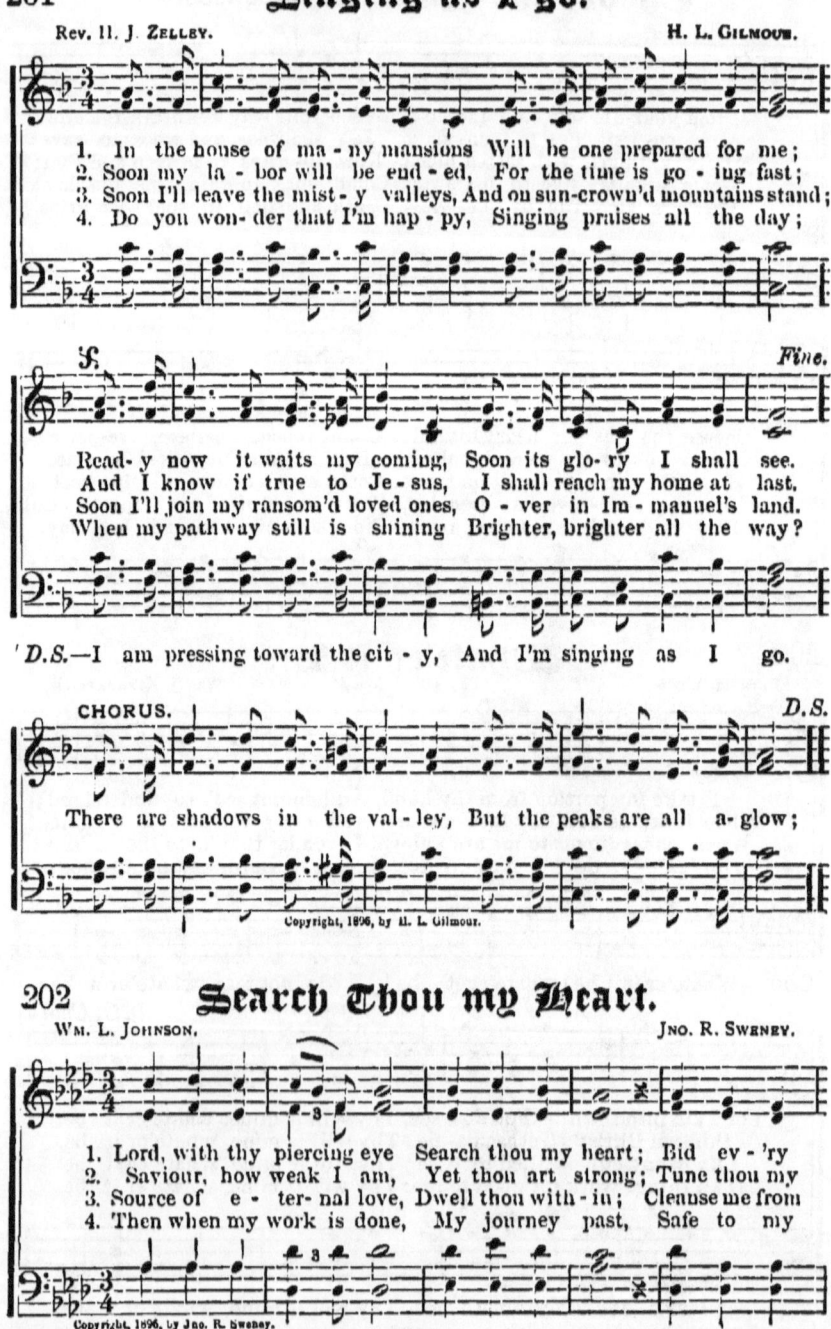

Deeper Yet.—CONCLUDED.

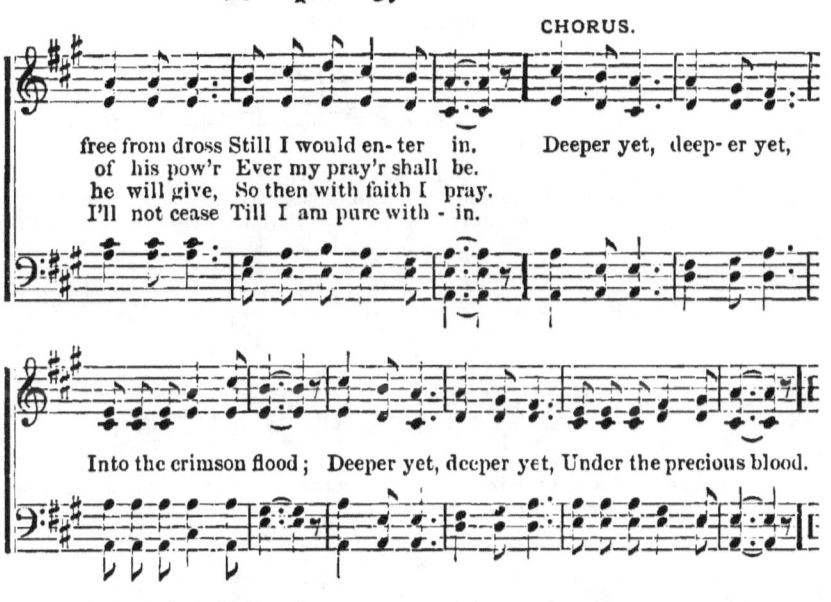

206 Old Jordan's Waves I do not Fear.

C. J. B.
CHAS. J. BUTLER.

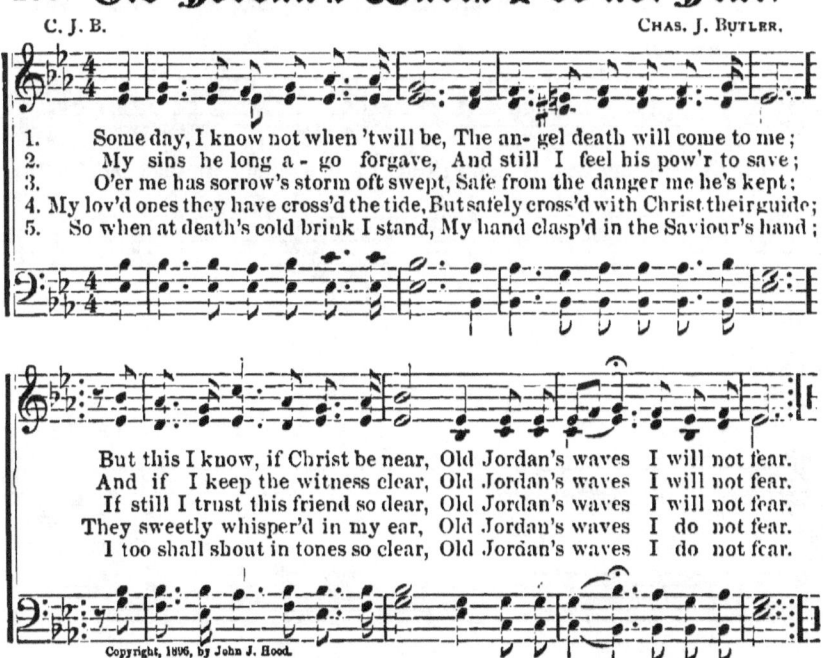

1. Some day, I know not when 'twill be, The an-gel death will come to me;
2. My sins he long a-go forgave, And still I feel his pow'r to save;
3. O'er me has sorrow's storm oft swept, Safe from the danger me he's kept;
4. My lov'd ones they have cross'd the tide, But safely cross'd with Christ their guide;
5. So when at death's cold brink I stand, My hand clasp'd in the Saviour's hand;

But this I know, if Christ be near, Old Jordan's waves I will not fear.
And if I keep the witness clear, Old Jordan's waves I will not fear.
If still I trust this friend so dear, Old Jordan's waves I will not fear.
They sweetly whisper'd in my ear, Old Jordan's waves I do not fear.
I too shall shout in tones so clear, Old Jordan's waves I do not fear.

Copyright, 1896, by John J. Hood.

207. My Beloved and Friend.

"This is my Beloved, and this is my Friend."—Canticles v: 16.

Virginia W. Moyer.   H. L. Gilmour.

1. The world may sing its siren song, May lure where love and laughter blend;
2. Though I may suffer loss and death, No human arm its strength may lend;
3. The judgment has no fears for me, I safe shall be when mountains rend;

It has no charm to win my soul, For Christ my Lover is, and Friend.
The bruised reed he will not break, For Christ my Lover is, and Friend.
My Lord is my suf-fi-ciency, And he my Lov-er is, and Friend.

D. S.—fairest to my inward gaze, My soul's enraptured with the sight.

CHORUS.

Oh, Christ is my Beloved and Friend; I lean on him with such delight, The

Copyright, 1895, by H. L. Gilmour.

208. Love Divine.

Charles Wesley.   Tune, LOVE DIVINE. 8,7, d.

1. Love di-vine, all love ex-cel-ling, Joy of heaven, to earth come down!

Love Divine.—CONCLUDED.

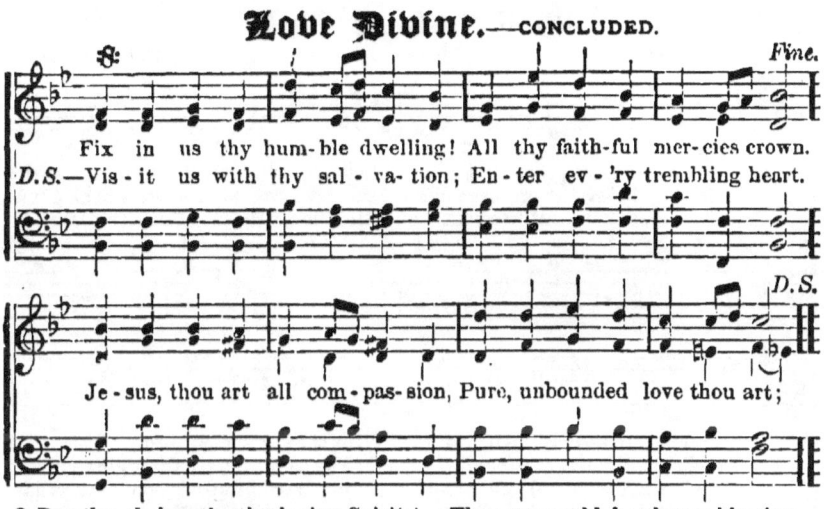

Fix in us thy hum-ble dwelling! All thy faith-ful mer-cies crown.
D.S.—Vis-it us with thy sal-va-tion; En-ter ev-'ry trembling heart.

Je-sus, thou art all com-pas-sion, Pure, unbounded love thou art;

2 Breathe, oh, breathe thy loving Spirit
Into every troubled breast!
Let us all in thee inherit,
Let us find that second rest.
Take away our bent to sinning;
Alpha and Omega be;
End of faith, as its beginning,
Set our hearts at liberty.

3 Come, almighty to deliver,
Let us all thy life receive;
Suddenly return, and never,
Never more thy temples leave;

Thee we would be always blessing,
Serve thee as thy hosts above,
Pray, and praise thee without ceasing,
Glory in thy perfect love.

4 Finish then thy new creation;
Pure and spotless let us be;
Let us see thy great salvation,
Perfectly restored in thee:
Changed from glory into glory,
Till in heaven we take our place,
Till we cast our crowns before thee,
Lost in wonder, love, and praise.

209 I'm Going Home.

Wm. Hunter, D. D. Arr. by Rev. W. McDonald.

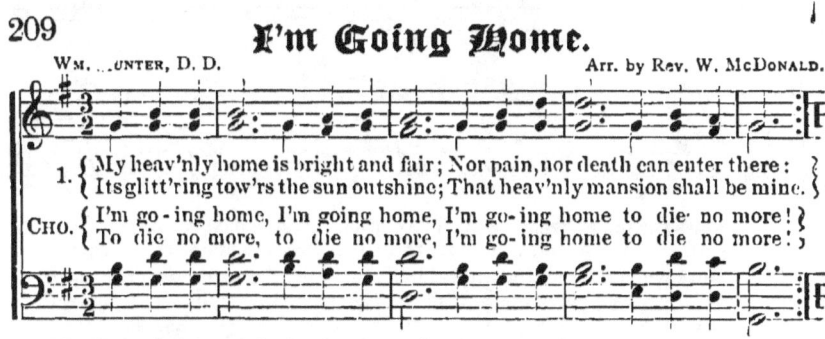

1. { My heav'nly home is bright and fair; Nor pain, nor death can enter there:
     Its glitt'ring tow'rs the sun outshine; That heav'nly mansion shall be mine. }

Cho. { I'm go-ing home, I'm going home, I'm go-ing home to die no more!
       To die no more, to die no more, I'm go-ing home to die no more! }

2 My Father's house is built on high,
Far, far above the starry sky:
When from this earthly prison free,
That heavenly mansion mine shall be.

3 While here, a stranger far from home,
Affliction's waves may round me foam
Although like Lazarus, sick and poor,
My heavenly mansion is secure.

4 Let others seek a home below,
Which flames devour, or waves o'er-
Be mine a happier lot to own   [flow,
A heavenly mansion near the throne.

5 Then fail this earth, let stars decline,
And sun and moon refuse to shine,
All nature sink and cease to be,
That heavenly mansion stands for me.

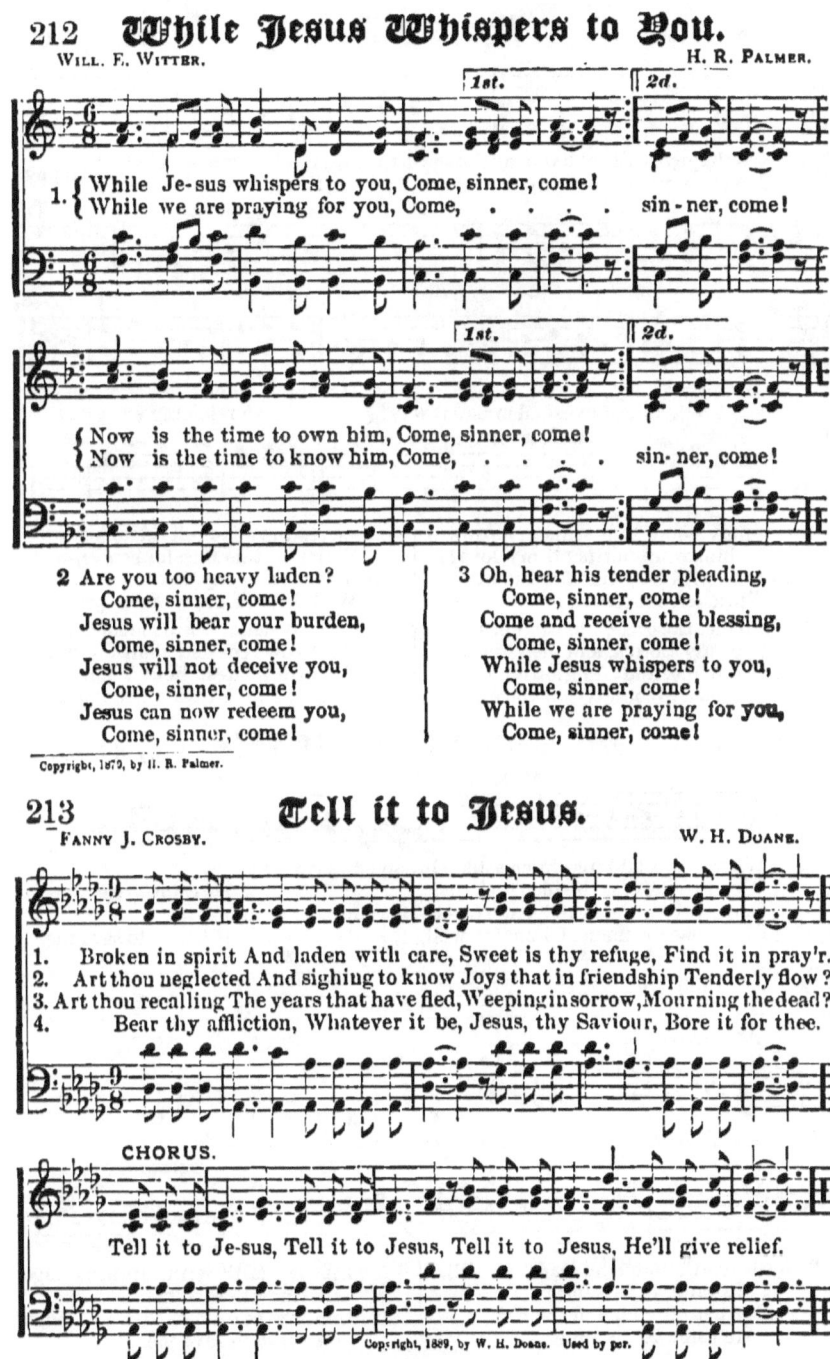

212. While Jesus Whispers to You.

WILL. F. WITTER. H. R. PALMER.

1. While Jesus whispers to you, Come, sinner, come!
   While we are praying for you, Come, ... sinner, come!
   Now is the time to own him, Come, sinner, come!
   Now is the time to know him, Come, ... sinner, come!

2 Are you too heavy laden?
   Come, sinner, come!
   Jesus will bear your burden,
   Come, sinner, come!
   Jesus will not deceive you,
   Come, sinner, come!
   Jesus can now redeem you,
   Come, sinner, come!

3 Oh, hear his tender pleading,
   Come, sinner, come!
   Come and receive the blessing,
   Come, sinner, come!
   While Jesus whispers to you,
   Come, sinner, come!
   While we are praying for you,
   Come, sinner, come!

Copyright, 1879, by H. R. Palmer.

213. Tell it to Jesus.

FANNY J. CROSBY. W. H. DOANE.

1. Broken in spirit And laden with care, Sweet is thy refuge, Find it in pray'r.
2. Art thou neglected And sighing to know Joys that in friendship Tenderly flow?
3. Art thou recalling The years that have fled, Weeping in sorrow, Mourning the dead?
4. Bear thy affliction, Whatever it be, Jesus, thy Saviour, Bore it for thee.

CHORUS.

Tell it to Jesus, Tell it to Jesus, Tell it to Jesus, He'll give relief.

Copyright, 1889, by W. H. Doane. Used by per.

214 Happy Day.

P. Doddridge. English Melody.

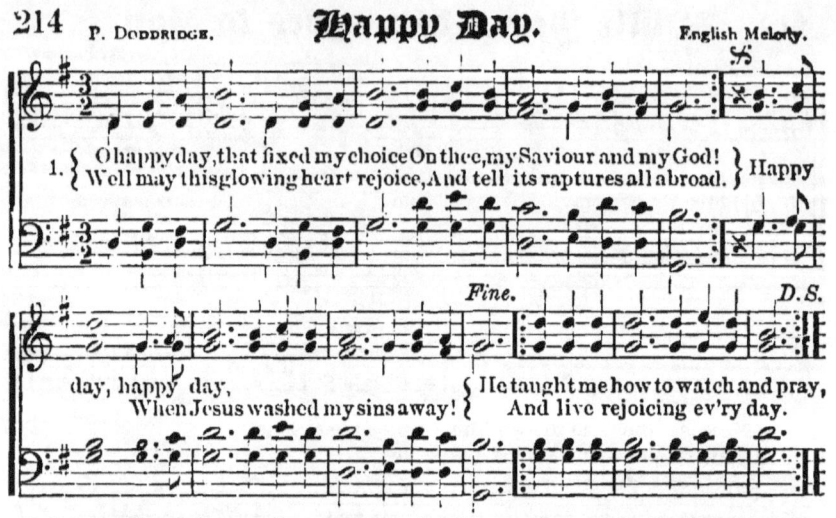

1. O happy day, that fixed my choice On thee, my Saviour and my God!
Well may this glowing heart rejoice, And tell its raptures all abroad.
Happy day, happy day, When Jesus washed my sins away!
He taught me how to watch and pray, And live rejoicing ev'ry day.

2 O happy bond, that seals my vows
  To him who merits all my love!
  Let cheerful anthems fill his house,
  While to that sacred shrine I move.

3 'Tis done! the great transaction's done!
  I am my Lord's, and he is mine:
  He drew me, and I followed on,
  Charmed to confess that voice divine.

4 Now rest, my long-divided heart;
  Fixed on this blissful center, rest;
  Nor ever from thy Lord depart;
  With him of every good possessed.

5 High heav'n that heard the solemn vow,
  That vow renewed shall daily hear,
  Till in life's latest hour I bow,
  And bless in death a bond so dear.

215 He Came to Save Me.

H F. Blair. Wm. J. Kirkpatrick.

1. When Jesus laid his crown aside, He came to save me;
When on the cross he bled and died, . . . He came to save me.
2. In my poor heart he deigns to dwell, He came to save me;
Oh, praise his name, I know it well, . . . He came to save me.

REFRAIN.
I'm so glad, I'm so glad, I'm so glad that Jesus came, And grace is free,
He . . . came to save me.

3 With gentle hand he leads me still,
  He came to save me;
  And trusting him I fear no ill,
  He came to save me.

4 To him my faith with rapture clings,
  He came to save me;
  To him my heart looks up and sings,
  He came to save me.

Copyright, 1885, by Wm. J. Kirkpatrick.

216. I'll Live for Him.
C. R. Dunbar

1. My life, my love I give to thee, Thou Lamb of God, who died for me;
2. I now believe thou dost receive, For thou hast died that I might live;
3. Oh, thou who died on Cal-va-ry, To save my soul and make me free,

Cho.—I'll live for him who died for me, How happy then my life shall be!

Oh, may I ev-er faith-ful be, My Sav-iour and my God!
And now henceforth I'll trust in thee, My Sav-iour and my God!
I con-se-crate my life to thee, My Sav-iour and my God!

I'll live for him who died for me, My Sav-iour and my God!

Copyright of R. L. Hudson, used by per.

217. He is Calling.
F. W. Faber.   Arr. by S. J. Vail.

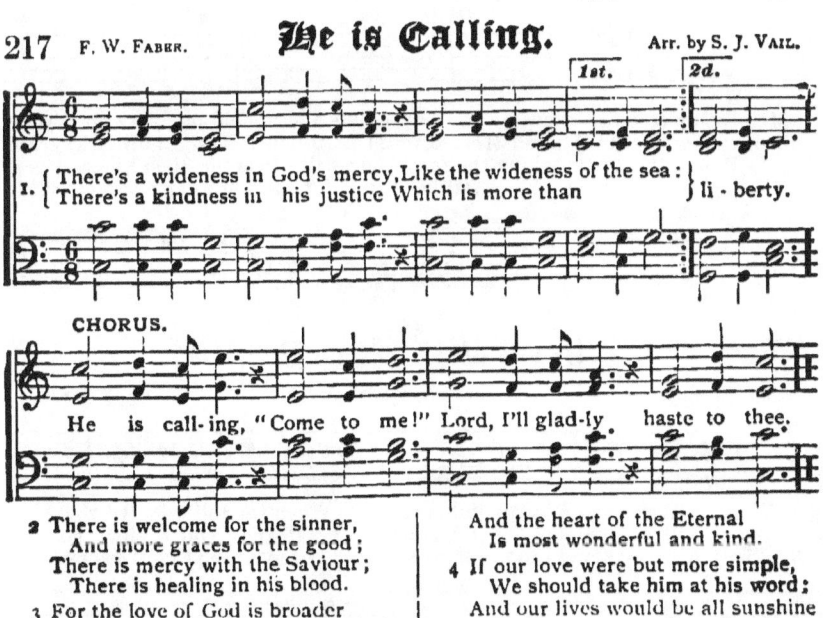

1. { There's a wideness in God's mercy, Like the wideness of the sea:
   { There's a kindness in his justice Which is more than } li-berty.

CHORUS.

He is call-ing, "Come to me!" Lord, I'll glad-ly haste to thee.

2 There is welcome for the sinner,
   And more graces for the good;
   There is mercy with the Saviour;
   There is healing in his blood.

3 For the love of God is broader
   Than the measure of man's mind;

And the heart of the Eternal
   Is most wonderful and kind.

4 If our love were but more simple,
   We should take him at his word;
   And our lives would be all sunshine
   In the sweetness of our Lord.

Love and Praise, 3—O

218. Moment by Moment.

E. E. Hewitt.
Wm. J. Kirkpatrick.

1. Moment by moment, as the sands fall, Moment by moment, life comes to all;
2. Moment by moment, led by thy hand, Truly obeying each wise command,
3. Moment by moment, hid in thy tow'r, Filled with thy Spirit, saved by thy pow'r,
4. Moment by moment, growing in grace, Growing in knowledge, till face to face,

So let thy life flow, Lord, into mine, Cleansing, transforming, keeping me thine;
Seeking thy precepts, learning thy will, By thine indwelling, pleasing thee still;
Sharing the pleasure, bearing the pain, Using the "talent," finding the gain,
In thy blest likeness, faultless and fair, Praising the mercy bringing me there.

Moment by moment, show me the way, Guide and uphold me; save me, I pray.
Moment by moment, till life shall cease, Teach me thy truth, Lord; grant me thy peace.
Doing the duty, taking the rest, Thou wilt direct me, thou knowest best.
Joy overflowing then shall be mine, Glory and blessing evermore thine.

Copyright, 1896, by Wm. J. Kirkpatrick.

219. Where will You Stand?

L. E. J.
(For Male Voices.)
L. E. Jones.

1. Where will you stand in the judgment day, When the roll is called above?
2. Where will you stand in the judgment day? Will the awful verdict be,
3. Where will you stand in the judgment day? O repent, on Christ believe;

Copyright, 1896, by John J. Hood.

221. The Morning Light.

SAMUEL F. SMITH. Tune, WEBB. 7, 6.

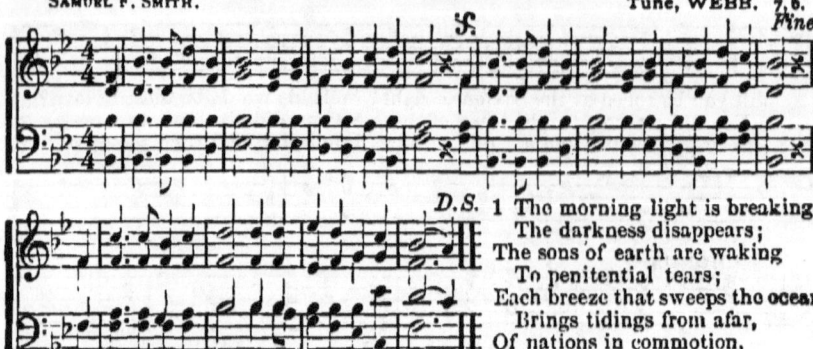

1 The morning light is breaking;
The darkness disappears;
The sons of earth are waking
To penitential tears;
Each breeze that sweeps the ocean
Brings tidings from afar,
Of nations in commotion,
Prepared for Zion's war.

2 See heathen nations bending
Before the God we love,
And thousand hearts ascending
In gratitude above;
While sinners, now confessing,
The gospel call obey,
And seek the Saviour's blessing,
A nation in a day.

3 Blest river of salvation,
Pursue thine onward way;
Flow thou to every nation,
Nor in thy richness stay:
Stay not till all the lowly
Triumphant reach their home;
Stay not till all the holy
Proclaim, "The Lord is come!"

222. Stand up, stand up for Jesus.

GEO. DUFFIELD, Jr. Tune above.

1 STAND up, stand up for Jesus,
Ye soldiers of the cross;
Lift high his royal banner,
It must not suffer loss;
From victory unto victory
His army shall he lead
Till every foe is vanquished
And Christ is Lord indeed.

2 Stand up, stand up for Jesus,
The trumpet call obey;
Forth to the mighty conflict,
In this his glorious day:
"Ye that are men, now serve him,"
Against unnumbered foes:
Your courage rise with danger,
And strength to strength oppose.

3 Stand up, stand up for Jesus,
Stand in his strength alone;
The arm of flesh will fail you;
Ye dare not trust your own:
Put on the gospel armor,
Each piece put on with prayer;
Where duty calls, or danger,
Be never wanting there.

4 Stand up, stand up for Jesus,
The strife will not be long;
This day the noise of battle,
The next the victor's song:
To him that overcometh,
A crown of life shall be;
He with the King of glory
Shall reign eternally.

223. Work, for the Night is Coming.

1 WORK, for the night is coming,
Work through the morning hours;
Work, while the dew is sparkling,
Work 'mid springing flowers;
Work, when the days grow brighter,
Work in the glowing sun;
Work, for the night is coming,
When man's work is done.

2 Work, for the night is coming,
Work through the sunny noon;
Fill brightest hours with labor,
Rest comes sure and soon,
Give every flying minute
Something to keep in store:
Work, for the night is coming,
When man works no more.

3 Work, for the night is coming,
Under the sunset skies;
While their bright tints are glowing,
Work, for daylight flies.
Work till the last beam fadeth,
Fadeth to shine no more;
Work while the night is darkening,
When man's work is o'er.

224. Jesus, the Light.
H. L. Gilmour. — Arr. by H. L. G.

1. Let my gaze be fixed on thee, Jesus, the light of the world;
As I look, new beauties see, Jesus, the light . . . of the world.

D.C.—Falling around us by day and by night,—Jesus, the light . . . of the world.

CHORUS.
Walk in the light, beautiful light, Come where the dew-drops of mercy are bright,

Copyright, 1893, by H. L. Gilmour.

2. Let my hands be strong for thee,
Jesus, the light of the world;
And my feet be swift and free,
Jesus, the light of the world.

3. When the tempter would alarm,
Jesus, the light of the world;
Bare, oh, bare thy mighty arm,
Jesus, the light of the world.

4. Walk the waves, across life's sea,
Jesus, the light of the world;
Nearer come, O Lord, to me,
Jesus, the light of the world.

5. Be a shelter in the storm,
Jesus, the light of the world;
Keep, oh, keep thy child from harm,
Jesus, the light of the world.

225. A Song of Praise.
E. E. Hewitt. — Arr. by W. J. K.

1. My heart uplifts a happy song, While tender rec-ollections throng;
2. Have sparkling sunbeams cheered the day, And roses bloomed along the way?
3. Or have the clouds o'erspread the sky, While at my feet the roses die?
4. Bright angels, sweep your harps of gold, But half his praise hath not been told;

And above the rest this note shall swell, This note shall swell, this note shall swell,

As sweet as bells that ring above, The strains that breathe my Saviour's love.
Let mem'ry each fair scene recall, And bless the Lord who sent them all.
Since Je-sus bore the cross for me, I'll trust him tho' I cannot see.
Come, all who my Redeem-er know, Still let the joy-ful mu-sic flow.

Copyright, 1894, by Wm. J. Kirkpatrick.

And above the rest this note shall swell, My Jesus hath done all things well.

Follow All the Way. —CONCLUDED.

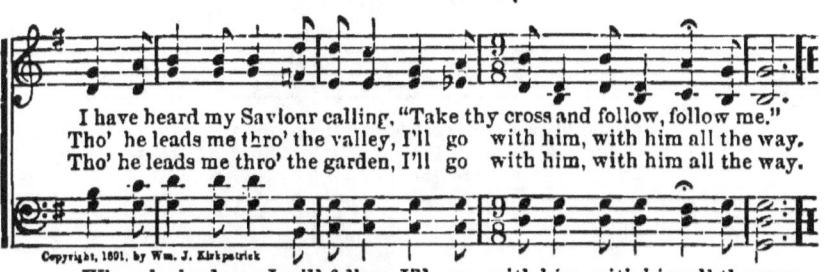

4 ‖: Tho' the path be dark and dreary, :‖
I'll go with him, with him all the way.

5 ‖: Tho' he leads me to the conflict, :‖
I'll go with him, with him all the way.

6 ‖: Tho' he leads through fiery trials, :‖
I'll go with him, with him all the way.

7 ‖: I will follow on to know him, :‖
He's my Saviour, Saviour, Brother, Friend.

8 ‖: He will give me grace and glory, :‖
He will keep me, keep me all the way.

9 ‖: O 'tis sweet to follow Jesus, :‖
And be with him, with him all the way.

228. The Golden Key.

"Prayer is the key to unlock the door, and the bolt to shut in the night."

D. K. W.   JNO. R. SWENEY.

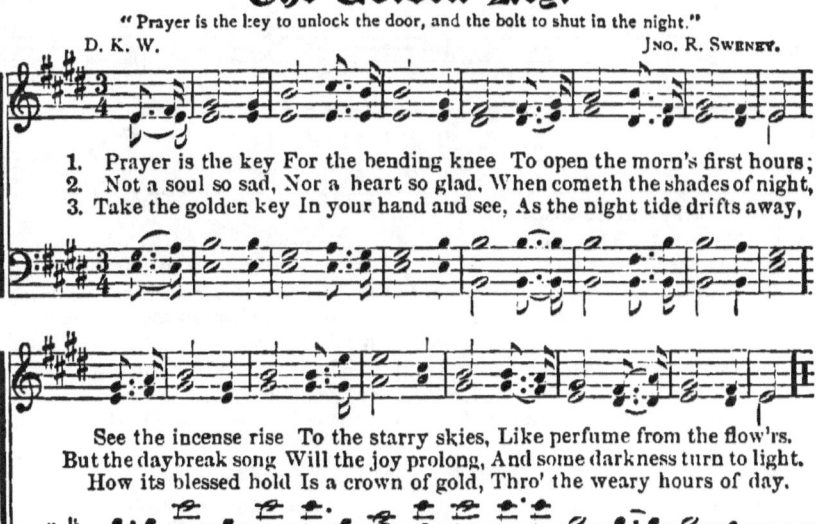

4 When the shadows fall,
And the vesper call
Is sobbing its low refrain,
'Tis a garland sweet
To the toil-dent feet,
And an antidote for pain.

5 Soon the year's dark door
Shall be shut no more:
Life's tears shall be wiped away,
As the pearl gates swing,
And the gold harps ring,
And the sun unsheathes for aye.

229. The Gospel Feast.

CHARLES WESLEY.
Cho. by H. L. G.
"Come, for all things are ready."
Luke xiv; 16.
H. L. GILMOUR. By per.

1. Come, sinners, to the gos-pel feast; It is for you, it is for me;
Let ev-'ry soul be Je-sus' guest; It is for you, it is for me.

2. Ye need not one be left behind, It is for you, it is for me;
For God hath bidden all mankind, It is for you, it is for me.

D.S.—O wea-ry wand'rer, come and see, It is for you, it is for me.

CHORUS.
Sal-vation full, sal-vation free, The price was paid on Cal-va-ry;

Copyright, 1889, by H. L. Gilmour.

3 Sent by my Lord, on you I call;
The invitation is to all:

4 Come, all the world! come, sinner, thou!
All things in Christ are ready now.

5 Come, all ye souls by sin oppressed,
Ye restless wanderers after rest;

6 Ye poor, and maimed, and halt, and blind
In Christ a hearty welcome find.

7 My message as from God receive;
Ye all may come to Christ and live:

8 O let this love your hearts constrain,
Nor suffer him to die in vain.

9 See him set forth before your eyes,
That precious, bleeding sacrifice:

10 His offered benefits embrace,
And freely now be saved by grace.

230. Awake, My Soul.

MEDLEY.
Tune, LOVING-KINDNESS. L. M

1. Awake, my soul to joyful lays, And sing thy great Redeemer's praise;
2. He saw me ru-ined in the fall, Yet loved me not-withstanding all;

Awake, My Soul.—CONCLUDED.

He just-ly claims a song from me, His lov-ing-kind-ness, oh, how free!
He saved me from my lost e-state, His lov-ing-kind-ness, oh, how great!

Lov-ing-kindness, lov-ing-kindness, His lov-ing-kind-ness, oh, how free!
Lov-ing-kindness, lov-ing-kindness, His lov-ing-kind-ness, oh, how great!

3 Though num'rous hosts of mighty foes,
Though earth and hell my way oppose,
He safely leads my soul along,
His loving-kindness, oh, how strong!

4 When trouble, like a gloomy cloud,
Has gathered thick, and thundered loud,
He near my soul has always stood,
His loving-kindness, oh, how good!

231 My Faith Looks Up to Thee.

RAY PALMER.   L. MASON.

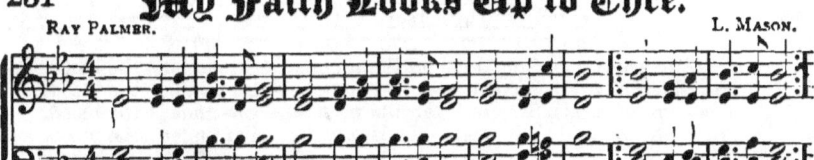

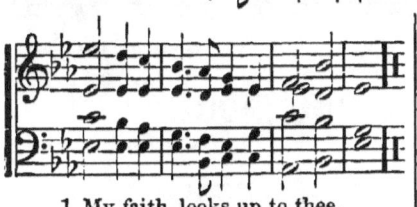

1 My faith looks up to thee,
Thou Lamb of Calvary,
Saviour divine!
Now hear me while I pray;
Take all my guilt away;
Oh, let me from this day
Be wholly thine!

2 May thy rich grace impart
Strength to my fainting heart,
My zeal inspire!
As thou hast died for me,
Oh, may my love to thee
Pure, warm, and changeless be—
A living fire!

3 While life's dark maze I tread,
And griefs around me spread,
Be thou my guide;
Bid darkness turn to day,
Wipe sorrow's tears away,
Nor let me ever stray
From thee aside.

4 When ends life's transient dream,
When death's cold sullen stream
Shall o'er me roll,
Blest Saviour! then, in love,
Fear and distrust remove;
Oh, bear me safe above—
A ransomed soul!

232. Step Out on the Promise.

MAGGIE POTTER. ARR. by E. F. M.
E. F. MILLER.

1. O mourner in Zi-on, how blessed art thou, For Je-sus is wait-ing to com-fort thee now, Fear not to re-ly on the word of thy God; Step out on the promise,—get under the blood.
2. O ye that are hun-gry and thirsty, re-joice! For ye shall be filled; do you hear that sweet voice In-vit-ing you now to the ban-quet of God? Step out on the promise,—get under the blood.
3. Who sighs for a heart from in-i-qui-ty free? O poor, troubled soul! there's a promise for thee, There's rest, weary one, in the bos-om of God; Step out on the promise,—get under the blood.
4. Step out on the promise, and Christ you shall win, "The blood of his Son cleanseth us from all sin," It cleanseth me now, hal-le-lu-jah to God! I rest on his promise,—I'm under the blood.

From "The Shout of Victory," by per

233. Bless the Lord, my Soul.

E. A. BARNES.
WM. J. KIRKPATRICK.

1. Oh, bless the Lord, my soul, As the friend who died for thee; And bless him
2. Oh, bless the Lord, my soul, As the rock in which we hide; And bless him
3. Oh, bless the Lord, my soul, As the hope so sure and sweet; And bless him
4. Oh, bless the Lord, my soul, As the guide in days to come; And bless him

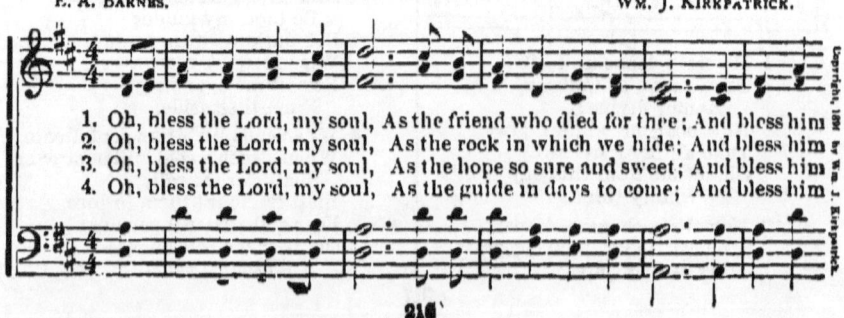

Bless the Lord, my Soul.—CONCLUDED.

234 E. Hopper. **Saviour, Pilot Me.** J. E. Gould.

1. Jesus, Saviour, pilot me
 Over life's tempestuous sea;
 Unknown waves before me roll,
 Hiding rock and treacherous shoal;
 Chart and compass came from thee:
 Jesus, Saviour, pilot me.

2. When the Apostles' fragile bark
 Struggled with the billows dark,
 On the stormy Galilee,
 Thou did'st walk across the sea;
 And when they beheld thy form,
 Safe they glided through the storm.

3. As a mother stills her child
 Thou canst hush the ocean wild;
 Boisterous waves obey thy will
 When thou say'st to them "Be still."
 Wondrous Sovereign of the sea,
 Jesus, Saviour, pilot me.

4. When at last I near the shore,
 And the fearful breakers roar
 'Twixt me and the peaceful rest,
 Then, while leaning on thy breast,
 May I hear thee say to me,
 "Fear not, I will pilot thee."

Antioch. C. M.

235 O for a thousand tongues.

1 O FOR a thousand tongues, to sing
My great Redeemer's praise;
The glories of my God and King,
The triumphs of his grace!

2 My gracious Master and my God,
Assist me to proclaim,
To spread through all the earth abroad,
The honors of thy name.

3 Jesus! the name that charms our fears,
That bids our sorrows cease;
'Tis music in the sinner's ears,
'Tis life, and health, and peace.

4 He breaks the power of canceled sin,
He sets the prisoner free;
His blood can make the foulest clean;
His blood availed for me.

5 He speaks, and, listening to his voice,
New life the dead receive;
The mournful, broken hearts rejoice;
The humble poor believe.

6 Hear him, ye deaf; his praise, ye dumb,
Your loosened tongues employ;
Ye blind, behold your Saviour come;
And leap, ye lame, for joy.

236 Joy to the world!

1 Joy to the world! the Lord is come;
Let earth receive her King;
Let every heart prepare him room,
And heaven and nature sing.

2 Joy to the world! the Saviour reigns;
Let men their songs employ;
While fields and floods, rocks, hills and
Repeat the sounding joy. [plains,

3 No more let sin and sorrow grow,
Nor thorns infest the ground;
He comes to make his blessings flow
Far as the curse is found.

4 He rules the world with truth and grace,
And makes the nations prove
The glories of his righteousness,
And wonders of his love.

237 The Lord's Prayer.

Reverently.

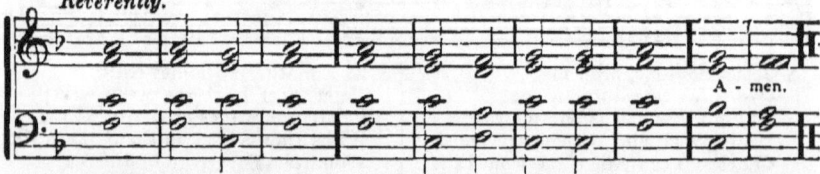

1. Our Father who art in heaven, hallowed | be thy | name, || Thy kingdom come, thy will be done in | earth, as-it | is in | heaven.

2. Give us this day our | daily | bread, || And forgive us our trespasses, as we forgive | them that | trespass a- | gainst us.

3. And lead us not into temptation, but deliver | us from | evil; || For thine is the kingdom, and the power and the | glory for- | ever and | ever. || A- | men.

INDEX.

Titles in CAPITALS; First lines in Roman type.

	HYMN.		HYMN.		HYMN.
Abiding in the	69	Come, sinners, to the	229	Hear the blessed invi-	181
A LIGHT AT THE RIV-	110	Come, s , to the living	71	Hear the voice of the	194
All glory to Jesus	54	Come to Jesus, wan-.	199	HE CAME TO SAVE ME	215
ALL O'ER THE WORLD	134	Come unto me, oh,	126	He gives me life,	164
ALL THE DAY LONG,	146	Come ye to the fount-	185	HE HIDETH MY SOUL	107
An offering now of	37	CONSECRATION,	177	HE IS ABLE TO DELIV-	7
Antioch, C. M.,	235	Conquering now, and	180	HE IS ALL IN ALL TO	2
Are you happy in	100			HE IS CALLING,	217
AS FAR AS THE EAST	8	DAY BY DAY,	167	HE IS MINE, I AM HIS	114
ASHAMED OF JESUS?	150	Dear Jesus, I am w.	51	He knows the bitter	211
A SHOUT OF VICTORY	162	DEEPER YET,	205	He leadeth his own	52
A SONG IN THE HEART	94	Down at the cross wh.	10	HE LEFT THE NINE-.	99
A SONG OF PRAISE,	225	Do you fear the foe	108	HE ROLLED THE SEA	156
AT MOTHER'S GRAVE	186	DRAW ME NEARER,	63	HE SAVES ME,	40
A voice is heard	46	DRINK OF THE WA-	185	HE WIPES THE TEAR	190
Awake, my soul,	230			HIS ANGER IS TURNED	82
Awake, slumbering h.	33	Encamped along the	20	HIS LOVING CALL,	126
A wonderful Saviour	107			HIS PROMISE I BE-	121
		FAITH IS THE VICTO-	20	HOMEWARD,	83
Bear the good tidings	134	Far away from home	186	Holy, great and glo-.	95
Be strong, O Chris-	125	Father, when shall	203	How oft in holy	149
Beyond the blue,	66	FOLLOW ALL THE	227	How restless the soul	47
Blessed assurance, Je-	168	For all the Lord has	22		
Blessed Lily of the v.	114	Forget not the num-.	120	I am coming to the c.	41
BLESSED REAPING, BY	135	FREELY MINE,	157	I AM GOING UP YON-.	111
BLESSED WAY,	68			I am praying, blessed	155
BLESS THE LORD, MY	233	GATHERING OUT OF	78	I am saved in Christ	62
BRIGHT, BEAUTIFUL	56	GATHER THE SHEAV.	130	I am thine, O Lord, I	63
Broken in spirit,	213	GLADLY WE WILL GO,	72	I am walking to-day	65
BROUGHT BACK,	47	Glory be to the Fath-	1	I do not ask to choose	89
BUILDING DAY BY D.	102	GLORIA PATRI,	1	I have a song I love to	9
By Samaria's wayside	34	GO AND TELL IT TO J.	132	I have heard my Sav-	227
		God sent his mighty	166	I know that my Re-.	151
CALLING YOU HOME,	79	God so loved the w.	189	I'LL BE WITH THEE,.	174
CHOOSE THE SAVIOUR	199	Go ye out in the high-	70	I'LL LIVE FOR HIM,	216
Christ has for sin	191			I'll sing of Jesus,	19
Christian soldiers,	6	HALLELUJAH, I'LL BE	178	I LOVE HIM FAR BET-	139
CHRIST IS COMING,	203	HALLELUJAH, I'M S.	149	I love the blessed	128
CHRIST OUR PASSO-	29	HALLELUJAH TO JE-	95	I love to tell the story	173
CHRIST'S INVITATION	194	HAPPY DAY,	214	I'm as happy as can	111
CHRIST WITHIN,	23	HAPPY IN A SAV-	109	I'M GOING HOME,	209
Come, contrite one,	84	Hark, 'tis the Master	124	I'm singing for Jesus	94
Come, Holy Ghost,	73	Have you, my dear	123	I must tell Jesus,	137
Come in, come in	88	HEAR AND ANSWER	155	I NEVER WILL CEASE	22

In that city, . . 77	Longing for the F. 113	On the way, . . 226
In that happy land 117	Lord, I'm coming h. 101	Onward, Christian . 197
In the blood from . 205	Lord, with thy pierc- 202	O Saviour, tarry yet . 220
In the hollow of . 62	Lost, lost on the m. . 140	O sinner, the Saviour 122
In the house of many 201	Love divine, all love 208	O sinner, won't you . 159
In the highways, . 70	Love found me, . 152	O 'tis blessed to be- . 68
In the Lord is our h.. 198		O to abide in Jesus, . 5
In the sunshine, . 44	Make me a blessing 89	Our blessed Redeem- 91
I shall be satisfied 145	Make way for the 33	Our Father which . 237
Is it nothing to . 91	March, march away, 26	Our friends on earth 196
I take my portion . 200	March on, march on, 162	Our Lamb is slain . 22
It pays to serve the 139	'Mid the toil and . 148	Out in the breakers . 170
It just suits me, . 31	Mighty army of the . 76	Out of shadow into . 121
I've a message from . 93	Moment by moment, 218	Overflowing meas- 24
I've a passport on . 174	More about Jesus, . 195	Over the dead line 122
I've heard of a Sav-. 74	My Advocate is on . 121	Over the river, . . 118
I've wandered far a-. 101	My beloved and F. 207	
I've yielded all for Je- 96	My body, soul, and . 177	Prayer is the key, 228
I will cling to the 28	My cup runneth o- 164	Pressed and run- . 24
I will go in the str. 39	My faith looks up to 231	Prevailing prayer 73
I will lift up mine . 157	My happy soul rejoic- 175	
I will shout his . 154	My heart uplifts a . 225	Rouse, ye christian,. 38
	My heart was once . 23	
Jesus, and shall it ev- 150	My heavenly home, . 209	Salvation's river,. 10
Jesus gives his peace 163	My life, my love I . 216	Saved to serve the M. 161
Jesus guides me all 131	My mother's Bible, 187	Saved to the utter- . 50
Jesus is calling for 56	My only interces- 115	Save one, . . . 170
Jesus is passing by, 84	My Saviour first . 138	Saviour, I belong to . 49
Jesus leads. . . 192	My soul in sad exile, 158	Saviour, I am com- . 153
Jesus lives, . . 76	My soul to-day is . 11	Saviour, I come in . 25
Jesus receiveth s.. 18		Saviour, lead me . 165
Jesus, Saviour, pilot 234	Not one forgotten 13	Saviour, pilot me,. 234
Jesus the light, . 224	Now, gracious Lord, 55	Search thou my h. . 202
Jesus will help y.. 43		See the ark of . . 42
Joy and light, . . 188	O blessed hope, so . 48	See the fields of . 130
Joy in service, . 51	O Eden, dear Eden 15	Send a cheer a- . 119
Joy to the world! the 236	O'er death's sea, in . 77	Send out the sunlight 87
Just ahead, . . 148	O for a heart that . 36	Shall I turn back? 140
Just a little music, . 141	O for a heart whit- 36	Shall we all meet a-. 143
Just lean upon Jesus, 86	O for a soul re- . 55	Since I have been . 9
Just over the ocean . 144	O for a thousand . 235	Sing a cheerful mar.. 127
	O happy day, that . 214	Singing as I go, . 201
Keep close to the 53	O, bless the Lord, 226,233	Sinner, O why do . 79
Kept in perfect p. 69	Oh, give me the rich 59	Some day, I know . 206
	Oh, I have some let-. 98	Sometime, . . 46
Lead me, Saviour,. 165	Oh, spread the tid- . 112	So tired of the life . 83
Leaning on the ev- 171	Oh, the best friend . 176	Speak to me, Jesus . 133
Leave not my soul 220	Oh, the joy of know- 45	Sprinkled with a-. 11
Let my gaze be . 224	Oh, the joy that . 30	Standing on the prom- 32
Letters from heav- 98	Oh, what wilt thou . 129	Stand up, stand up . 222
Let the sunshine . 108	Oh, wondrous Rock,. 35	Steer our bark away, 78
Lift your heart to Je- 60	O Lamb of God, most 210	Step out on the p.. 232
Living by the mo- . 97	Old Jordan's waves 206	Stepping in the l.. 51
Like a shepherd ten- 192	O Lord, I will praise 82	Sunshine in the s.. 12
Live like the blessed 16	O mourner in Zion, . 232	Sweet heaven, . 168
Live like the Mas- 16	Only a fond old . 92	
Look and live, . 93	On that morning br. 178	Taste and see, . 181

INDEX.

Tell it out with G.	100	The Same old way, 136
Tell it to Jesus, .	213	The Saviour is call-. 43
Tell the glad sto-	123	The sheep were sleep- 99
Tell the whole wide .	104	The story of won-. 189
Thank God, I see, .	19	The sweet Beulah 65
That old, old sto-.	172	The true riches, . 59
The banquet hall is .	18	The very same Je-. 71
The best friend is J	176	The way our fathers 136
The Comforter has	112	The world may sing, 207
The dear loving Sav-	40	They are pushing out 119
The golden now, .	204	They'll soon be . 4
The golden key, .	228	This life is like a . 53
The gospel feast, .	229	Tho' my sins were . 184
The grand old ark	42	Tho' numbered with 115
The great white t.	128	Tho' your sins be as. 182
The happy song, .	30	'Tis burning in my 166
The haven of rest,	158	'Tis everything to 90
The heaven-bound	75	'Tis the grandest th.. 7
The heavenly Pi-.	81	Trying to walk in the 57
The home where .	116	
The joy of know-.	45	Under the cross, . 41
The latch of Fa-.	92	Unspeakably pre-. 3
The living fount is .	153	Unspeakable joy, . 54
The Lord is our Shep-	72	
The Lord's prayer,	237	Victory every- . 6
The love of God .	90	Victory shall be ours 14
The morning light is	221	Victory thro' gr. . 180
The old fountain,.	34	Victory thro' Je-. 14
There are heights .	113	
There is a calm for .	4	
There is an hour .	204	Wait and murmur. 116
There is a refuge, .	64	Walking with Jesus, 146
There is constant joy	2	Wash me, O Lamb . 103
There is no one l.	179	Washed white as . 184
There's a dear, pre-.	187	We are almost h. . 144
There's a deep, silent	110	We are building in . 102
There's a hand held.	61	We are building on . 67
There's a hill lone .	106	We are soldiers of 127
There's a land unseen	15	We have an anchor 17
There's a wideness in	217	We shall see him,. 58
There's a wonderful.	172	Well I remember the 160
There's a word of .	13	We'll never say . 196
There's power in J.	175	What a fellowship, . 171
There's sunshine in .	12	What a meeting that 21

What a wond'f'l S.	191
What a wonderful .	81
Whate'er it be, .	200
What praises shall I	167
What vessel are you	75
When for me the sun-	80
When I shall wake .	145
When Israel out of .	156
When Jesus comes .	85
When Jesus laid his	215
When life's billows .	28
When my heart is sad	169
When my life work .	138
When on clouds of g.	27
When our march is .	117
When out in sin .	152
When sore afflictions	190
When the bride-g.	183
When the curtains .	142
When the people of .	58
When to the Sav- .	8
When wearied and b.	8
Where his voice is	124
Where will you stand	219
While Jesus whispers	211
While we walk by. .	109
Who can wash a sin-	179
Who will follow Je-.	147
Who will labor for .	135
Will Jesus find us	85
Will our lamps be .	183
Will you come to Je-.	193
Will your anchor h. .	17
Winning souls for	38
Withhold not thy h..	105
With Jesus in the ves-	81
Wonderful love that	56
Wonderful peace,	163
Wondrously saved	87
Work for the night is	223
Would you lose your	132
You ask what makes	154
You will find me in .	44

NEW MUSIC BOOKS, Etc

Three excellent hymn books in one volume—The

SACRED TRIO,

COMPRISING

Redemption Songs, Joyful Sound, Showers of Blessing.

Price, music edition, 85 cents by mail, Words edition, $15 per 100.

UNFADING TREASURES,

By SWENEY, KIRKPATRICK, & O'KANE. Every piece in this collection has been tried and found worthy.—A strong book! Will give great satisfaction.

Price, 35 cents per copy, by mail; $3.60 per dozen, at store.

For the Primary Department.

DEW DROPS.

Contains many interesting Services, also about 100 new songs for the little ones. By E. E. HEWITT, J. R. SWENEY, and WM. J. KIRKPATRICK.

Price, by mail, 25 cents.

LIVING HYMNS,

Compiled by Hon. JNO. WANAMAKER, assisted by JNO. R. SWENEY.

For the Sabbath School, Christian Endeavor Meeting, etc.—352 Pages.

Price, 50 cents, $4.80 per doz. Word edition $15 per 100; Orders of Worship $3 per 100.

Infant Praises,

by J. R. SWENEY and W. J. KIRKPATRICK. Easy, taking Music for the Primary Department.——Very popular.

Price, 25 cents, $2.40 per dozen.

SONGS OF LOVE AND PRAISE. NO. 2.

By SWENEY, KIRKPATRICK and GILMOUR, is the latest of a long series of admirable collections of sacred melody issued from year to year by these giants of song. The present work has over one hundred NEW pieces, also a selection of the well known favorites. 224 pages.

Price, 35 cents per copy, by mail; $3.60 per dozen, at store.

In their seasons we issue

New Song Services,

For Easter, Christmas, Childrens' Day, Thanksgiving, etc.

Send for the latest; three different services for any season mailed for 10 cents.

THE ORGAN SCORE ANTHEM BOOK, NO. 2.

By J. R. SWENEY and W. J. KIRKPATRICK. This collection will be welcomed by all choristers who have used "Anthems and Voluntaries," "The Banner Anthem Book," etc., by the same well-known authors. It has 67 anthems, etc.

Price, 60 cents per copy, by mail; $5.00 per dozen, at store.

The Finest of the Wheat,

By C. C. MCCABE, GEO. D. ELDERKIN, and others.

A very popular collection of the finest Sacred Melodies. 500,000 sold.

Price, 35 cents per copy; $3.60 per dozen.

Sample copies of above mailed on receipt of retail price.

PHILADELPHIA: 1024 Arch St.   **JOHN J. HOOD,**   CHICAGO: 940 W. Madison St.

www.ingramcontent.com/pod-product-compliance
Lightning Source LLC
Chambersburg PA
CBHW022016220426
43663CB00007B/1101